The
Jenny Craig Story

The
Jenny Craig Story

How One Woman Changes Millions of Lives

Jenny Craig

John Wiley & Sons, Inc.

Published by John Wiley & Sons, Inc., Hoboken, New Jersey.
Published simultaneously in Canada.

For general information on our other products and services, or technical support, please contact our Customer Care Department within the United States at 800-762-2974, outside the United States at 317-572-3993 or fax 317-572-4002.

Wiley also publishes its books in a variety of electronic formats. Some content that appears in print may not be available in electronic books.

For more information about Wiley products, visit our web site at www.wiley.com.

Library of Congress Cataloging-in-Publication Data:
Craig, Jenny.
    The Jenny Craig story: how one woman changes millions of lives / Jenny
Craig.
        p. cm.
Published simultaneously in the U.S. and Canada.
Includes index.
    ISBN 0-471-47864-4 (cloth)
    1. Craig, Jenny. 2. Businesswomen—United States—Biography.
3. Weight loss. 4. Reducing diets. 5. Jenny Craig, Inc. I. Title.
RM222.2.C7173 2004
338.7'616132'50973—dc22   2003021822

Printed in the United States of America.

10   9   8   7   6   5   4   3   2   1

To my children, whose love has been a pillar of support throughout my life as a parent. They continue to make me proud of them and of the wonderful parents they have become.

To my grandchildren, for not only have they brought immeasurable joy into my life, they represent a generation who are still young enough to design and shape a life that has meaning, community involvement, and personal fulfillment. My hope is that they will lead the way.

Acknowledgments

I would like to thank Patti Larchet for her help in searching through the company archives to retrieve photos and dates in order to accurately describe life in the Jenny Craig organization. I would also like to thank: Lisa Talamini, for her help in providing information on current changes within the company; Virginia Hood, my assistant for searching through my personal collection of thousands of photographs in order to find the right ones to include in this book; Jim Mallen (our former CFO), for helping me recall certain facts that happened long ago; and Marvin Sears (our attorney), for helping to provide with accuracy whatever ramifications there were resulting from legal action. Thanks to Debra Englander (my editor) for first giving me the confidence to continue writing this book and for believing that what I had to say would give inspiration to others. Most of all, I want to give thanks to the many clients whose successes have left vivid images that remind me daily of what my work has accomplished over these past 45 years. Your letters have been a constant source of joy and pride. Last, but certainly not least, I'd like to thank Sid for his support and love as a partner in business as well as in life. I thank you all for being such an influential part of my life.

JENNY CRAIG

Contents

CONTENTS

The
Jenny Craig Story

Introduction

This book began as a journal for my children and grandchildren, who have been asking me for years to write my life story so they'll have something to share with their own children and grandchildren. I didn't think my life was all that remarkable: I'm just appreciative of the happiness and success I've achieved. But a few years ago, when I had stepped down from the day-to-day running of Jenny Craig, Inc., I decided to appease my family since I finally had some spare time. I started jotting down random thoughts about my childhood, marriages, and career. Then friends and former colleagues started asking me what I was doing now that I was no longer president and chief operating officer (COO) of our $350 million company. When I told them I had put pen to paper, they encouraged me to tell the whole story of how Jenny Craig, Inc., came to be, more than 20 years ago.

I had already written four books, *Cutting Through the Fat, No Diet Required, Simple Pleasures,* and *What Have You Got to Lose?* Even though these books were successful (my first book was a *Wall Street Journal* and *USA Today* best-seller within a few weeks of its release, and it sold more than 400,000 copies), they were very different from this book. Those were cookbooks that I wrote to help our clients with their weight-management goals and to offer even more variety than the 70 plus food products that Jenny Craig, Inc., provides.

1

This time, I wanted to write something inspirational, because at Jenny Craig, Inc., all of our home-office staff, field employees, and franchisees share a common vision: to help change clients' lives as we support them along their weight-loss journeys. We literally have *living proof* of the efficacy of the program and the power of a positive attitude. Tens of thousands of satisfied clients have achieved their weight-loss goals and improved their lives because of a healthier approach to nutrition and exercise, a more balanced lifestyle, increased self-confidence, and higher self-esteem. Self-image affects every facet of our lives, our careers, our family relationships, our interactions with others, and our basic values and beliefs.

I truly believe "it's never too late"—for *anything* one wants to do, whether it is to lose weight, create a healthy lifestyle, find true love, or start a business. There are many people in the world who face some kind of physical challenge (whether it is obesity or something else), and there are many people who have had business dreams and thought maybe they were too old or didn't know enough to start a business. But *I'm* living proof that it can be done. I started Jenny Craig, Inc., with my second husband, Sid Craig, when I was 50 years old. Moreover, we started the company in Australia—a place we had never been before we opened our first weight-loss centers there!

The company we founded is now one of the largest weight-management service companies in the world, with more than 660 company-owned and franchised locations in the United States, Canada, Australia, New Zealand, Puerto Rico, and Guam. In 1988, *Inc.* magazine listed us as the sixth-fastest-growing privately held company in the United States (we went public in 1992 and private again in 2002). Our company is a household name, we're one of the most recognized names in weight management, and we're one of the strongest retail brands in the United States and abroad.

During my early years, as well as in my many years in business, I have always faced obstacles with the attitude that with enough determination, commitment, and perseverance, anything is possible. Within these pages, I have tried to give the reader a vivid picture of what life was like growing up after the Great Depression. I have shared some of the personal experiences as well as the challenges I have faced both in business and in my personal life, including a physical disability that changed the course of my life.

Over the years, clients and staff members have asked me numerous questions about how I started in the weight-management business, how the company developed, how we handled particular business challenges, and why the Jenny Craig program is so successful. I've tried to answer all of those questions as well as give a detailed account of the experiences Sid and I have shared while working together for 20 years as partners in business and in life. They have also asked why we chose to start the Jenny Craig company in Australia after having other weight-loss companies in America for 24 years. In addition to answering that question, I wanted to give a glimpse of Australia and its people, so that each reader can learn what a wonderful country it is and how Sid and I enjoyed two of the best years of our life together while living there.

There were many changes that took place both within the company and in the industry. Some of them had serious ramifications. Other changes were just part of developing and growing a business. Perhaps some of these same things happened in your business or in your life. When couples work together and put their heart and soul into a business, it's sometimes difficult to determine where business ends and family life begins.

I also hope that, throughout this book, there will be words that act to inspire you to be all that you can be and to erase "I can't do that" from your mental vocabulary.

I have enjoyed writing this book because it stimulated my memory of journeys that have evolved into a wonderful life. When people ask me if I have any regrets, I think to myself, "My only regret is that I don't have 70 more years to enjoy the unimaginable wonders of the future."

3

When I first agreed to go public with this book, I thought, "As an avid reader, what would *I* want to read about that would have meaning to me?" I have tried to include things that I think will interest you.

One of the things I hope to accomplish by examining behavior within our organization is to point out internal pitfalls that can make or break any company. I have learned that it's not what you *know*, it's what you *do* with what you know that makes the difference. Many people spend half a lifetime poring over books looking for answers, and once they find them, they do nothing with the information. Within these pages, I talk about specific incidents where key people received daily production figures, looked at them, dismissed them, and filed them away with no plan of action to improve them. Production figures are nothing more than symbols on a page. They are *meant* to supply information that requires action.

Many years ago, I was told that without a college degree I would always be an employee. Thank God they were wrong. While I truly believe in education for the sake of enriching one's life, if a formal education guaranteed success in business, then every Ph.D. would be a successful entrepreneur. Education does not have to take place in a classroom setting alone. There is a lot to be said for the school of hard knocks. Each of us has the opportunity to educate ourselves every day. When given a choice between a formally educated person and one with experience and street smarts, I'll choose the latter anytime.

So, if a little Cajun girl with no college degree can build a company that has more than 600 locations worldwide, with revenues of more than $350 million annually, just imagine what you can accomplish!

1

Early Years

"I learned very early that work was not a dirty four-letter word."

I guess I should start at the beginning. I was born Genevieve Marie Guidroz to Gertrude Acosta and James Yoric Guidroz on August 7, 1932, in Berwick, Louisiana, a little town about 100 miles south of New Orleans. I am the youngest of six children—two boys, Edwin James ("Bobby") and Leonard Louis (nicknamed "Red" because of the color of his hair), and four girls: Verna Louise, Elsie Rita, Gertrude Marie ("Trudy"), and me. We were all born approximately two years apart, with Verna being the firstborn, followed by Bobby, Elsie, Red, Trudy, and me, in that order.

I grew up in New Orleans. It was not the best of times economically for our country, because we were still suffering from the Great Depression. For our family, necessities were scarce and luxuries were not an option, to say the least. That condition was not due to a lack of ambition or hard work on my father's part, but instead was a result of the times. There were periods when Daddy held three jobs at once in order to keep the wolf away from the door. He worked as a carpenter, a bartender, a riverboat pilot, and a laborer unloading cargo boats on the riverfront. I remember one of his bosses coming

5

for dinner at our home. I sat there listening as he told my mother, "I wish I had 20 more workers like Mose—he does the work of *three men*." Daddy was always known as Captain Mose; no one called him by his given name, including my mother. He could navigate the narrowest waterways and dock a boat as easily as we park our cars. Perhaps that explains how he earned the moniker "Captain Mose."

Daddy often reminded us later in life of those hard times. He'd say, "People often refer to the 'good ole days' when one could buy a pound of beans for a nickel and a telephone call cost a nickel . . . but what they fail to remember is that no one had the nickel!" I guess that was the bad news of my early days, but it was also partly the good news in my development and work ethic. I learned very early that *work* was not a dirty four-letter word. Work not only provided people subsistence, but also gave them a sense of pride and accomplishment.

I find it interesting that by today's standards we would have been considered to be poor. Yet, I don't ever recall feeling poor or disadvantaged. There was nothing else to compare our lifestyle to; everyone we knew was in the same boat.

The phrase "keeping up with the Joneses" was introduced after World War II when most people were trying to build a new life for themselves. Displaying bigger and better material possessions was a way of telling your neighbors, "Look at me, I'm successful." In the early days of my youth, the "Joneses" were no better off than the Smiths or the Johnsons, not in *my* neighborhood anyway.

New Orleans has always been a city that is steeped in tradition. Celebrating Mardi Gras is one of those traditions that people practiced from early childhood. It was my favorite holiday, because we got to enjoy it for a whole week. As children, we would walk to Canal Street to watch each evening parade and catch beads and doubloons that were thrown from the colorful floats by costumed and masked revelers. Our house was about five miles from Canal Street, but walking with a large group of friends was so much fun that it seemed much shorter. I can remember each of us watching the parades and yelling, "Throw me something, *mister*," never really knowing if the costumed and masked person on the float was male or female. It is the common cry of all parade watchers hoping to take home a cache of treasures as proof of their success.

Another custom of the Mardi Gras season was the "king cake" party. Starting in early January, each month someone in our circle of friends would invite us to a party and serve a cake that had a tiny doll hidden inside. The person who unexpectedly got the doll had to give the next party. The cakes are shaped like a racetrack oval, with multicolored icing on top; some are made with cream cheese and/or fruit fillings that are quite delicious. Many of the local bakeries produce these cakes as they are part of a much-practiced celebration and are in great demand. The tradition of king cake parties would continue throughout each month until Mardi Gras day. Although I enjoyed the parties and I loved eating the cakes, with each bite, I can remember praying that I wouldn't get the doll so I wouldn't have to give the next party, because I knew my family could ill afford the extra cost.

Even though it was not the best of times, I still have many fond memories of the years we spent there. It was a real neighborhood. We all knew each other and were there to offer support when needed.

And in spite of the hard work my father had to endure, I never heard him once complain or present a "poor me" attitude. It was our custom to always have dinner together as a family every day. When Daddy came home from work, he would wash up, then kiss each one of us; then we would sit down at the table and talk about the happenings of the day. He was always interested in what we learned in school. I think one of the reasons he was so determined for us to get good educations was that he never had much of a formal education. In spite of the fact that his mother had taught school and was an avid student of Shakespeare (thus explaining his middle name *Yoric*), he never got to benefit from her formal education.

When his father was killed in World War I, he and his older brother had to leave school to support the family. I believe Daddy was in eighth grade at the time. I don't believe his mother spent much time continuing his education. What he learned, he learned on his own.

I find it sad that Daddy didn't have the benefit of a formal education, because he was very intelligent and he would have been a bright student. He could do math in his head quicker than anyone I've known. We would give him three or four figures to add, subtract, or multiply, and in an instant he'd give us the answer. He also proved to be an astute businessman later in life. At one time or another he owned restaurants, bars, and shrimp boats, and he leased crew boats to the oil companies. He was also an accomplished boat captain.

While we sat at the table recounting our experiences of the day, my mother was busy warming the food she had cooked earlier. She was always sure to have dinner ready when he got home, partly because sometimes dinner was between Daddy's jobs and he had little time to eat, and partly because my father was a taskmaster. He demanded certain things of his household. Having dinner ready when *he* was ready was one of them. Many times I heard my mother say to him, "You're working so hard I worry about you," and his standard reply was, "Hard work never killed anybody," a phrase that is ingrained in my subconscious. I grew up believing that if you didn't work hard, you would die young (a concept with some credibility).

> I grew up believing that
> if you didn't work hard,
> you would die young.

I have always been grateful for the early lessons I learned about the value of work. I attribute any success I have achieved to my willingness to do whatever it takes to get the job done. I don't believe I'm smarter or more talented than most people, but I can work as hard and as long as the best of them.

> ## I attribute any success I have achieved to my willingness to do whatever it takes to get the job done.

I believe that most people today work only for the material benefits and miss or ignore the true enjoyment of doing something that is productive and that builds character. Image and ego seem to be the driving forces behind many achievers today. I don't mean to generalize but only to point out the difference in attitudes that develop as a result of the times, the opportunities available, and the rewards they offer. So in many ways my attitude toward work was developed at a very young age. My husband Sid has often said to me, "You were bred to work." Perhaps he's right.

> ## I don't believe I'm smarter or more talented than most people, but I can work as hard and as long as the best of them.

Among many values I learned while growing up is the value of honesty. My dad hated a liar. If someone he knew lied, he'd say, "That guy would rather climb a tree to tell a lie than stand on the ground and tell the truth," meaning, of course, that the man went out of his way to lie. As children and as adults, we could never lie to my father. Knowing how he felt and looking into his eyes, we could tell that truth was our only option.

In those days, parents didn't have to consult books to know how and when to discipline their children. The criteria were simple: If you exhibited wrong or unacceptable behavior, expect consequences. To say that my father was strict would be like saying the Pacific Ocean is a small pond. There were rules in the household and we knew better than to break them.

I believe that most people today
work only for the material benefits
and miss or ignore the true enjoyment of
doing something that is productive
and that builds character.

We all had chores that we regularly did without question. Trudy and I were responsible for clean dishes. After each evening meal, we would wash and dry the dishes. We took turns as to who washed and who dried. There was never a discussion about *if* we should do it, only *who* did what. My brother Red was responsible for taking out the garbage and for cutting the grass. Elsie did a lot of the ironing and mending. Verna helped Mama with the washing, which was done with the old wringer-type washing machine, and the only dryer was the outside clothesline. Household chores were not so automated in those days, and although washing and cleaning took many more hours, there were some benefits. I still love the smell of wind-dried linens that have been kissed by sunshine.

Despite the rules and as strict as my dad was, we all knew we were loved. And only once did I see my father strike one of his children. One day when he was returning home in between jobs, he passed my brother Red's school. There was Red sitting in the yard smoking. Daddy didn't do anything then, but later that evening he asked Red if he had been smoking and Red answered, "No, sir." My father then told him what he had seen and gave him a chance to reconsider his answer.

After Red admitted he had smoked "just to see what it was like," Daddy took him into the bathroom, pulled down his pants, and gave him a spanking. I could hear the whacks as I stood outside the bathroom door crying because I thought Daddy would hurt him. Later Red said the only thing Daddy hurt was his pride. I think deep down the spanking was more for lying than for smoking because, to Daddy, lying was the most unforgivable sin. Obviously this incident left a lasting impression even though it didn't happen to me.

Actually, Daddy was very proud of his family. I don't ever remember having a baby-sitter. My parents took us everywhere they went, all six of us. And we all had to perform whenever we visited a friend's home. Elsie would sing solo (she had a beautiful voice). She sang on the radio for the 7-Up program. Red would tap-dance "Two Tickets to Georgia," then Trudy and I would close the act with a duet of "God Bless America." We all still laugh at what the audience must have thought. They probably said, "Oh God, here come those untalented Guidroz kids again," but we never guessed it at the time. We had fun, we were happy to be included in all the activities, and we appreciated the accolades of encouragement, even if they were false. It helps to understand that there was very little available to entertain people in those days. Catching fireflies could happily occupy an entire evening. So I guess even bad entertainment was endurable.

In any case, having to perform was good training for me because as a result I have never feared public speaking as I understand most people do. When my children were young, they saw me singing and dancing alone throughout the house and judging by their laughter and the looks they gave me, they must have thought their mother was strange. I still love to sing and dance! Like all kids, I was motivated by what I saw in the movies: I could see myself as the kind of woman in roles played by Katharine Hepburn and Hedy Lamarr. Those women always had gorgeous silk gowns and silk bed linens, and I thought, "Oh, that looks so beautiful—one day I'm going to have those." And I have fulfilled that dream.

There's nothing specific I can remember about what I wanted to be when I grew up. I don't think women then even considered the kinds of careers that women have today. And the same is true of me. I don't think even my mother could have envisioned the extent of my success, because women just weren't in business in those days—business careers for women were just nonexistent. Society has evolved to such an extent that now they have become the norm.

I do remember that when I was really little, I told Mama I would like to be a nun, and I saw her eyes light up. I think nothing would have pleased her more than to have one of her children as a member of the Church. Ours was a very Catholic household: My mother had a small altar, and every day she would kneel before it and pray. She attended Mass every Sunday and every holy day of obligation. Of course, we children all went along. She insisted we attend Catholic school and practice good Christian values.

Sometimes Trudy and I would pretend to be nuns and pin a towel on our heads to resemble a nun's habit. We would then pretend to teach school, because all our teachers were nuns, and we figured that that was their only role in life. Sometimes we pretended the other did something naughty, and we reprimanded each other with a ruler whack on the knuckles. My aspirations of becoming a nun changed once I discovered boys were not just pesky little dorks but were kind of cute.

I also liked to ride horses, so maybe I saw myself as Dale Evans. At one time, I thought I might be a singer on the stage like Ethel Merman. I didn't have a belting, booming voice like she did, but I thought maybe it would develop as I got older! Even now, when Sid and I go to the Derby in Kentucky and everyone sings "My Old Kentucky Home," people sometimes turn to me and say, "Gee, you have a nice voice." I still like to sing, but the only singing I do now is at the races and at Christmastime, singing carols.

Sometimes my own children question me about my childhood. My failure to respond with a lot of detailed accounts of my life back then prompts them to think I just don't wish to revisit those years. What they don't understand is that life was so mundane and unmemorable that there weren't many events that left lasting impressions. Any memories I do have are all of a happy childhood.

When I was growing up, we didn't take exotic trips or go to places like Universal City, Disneyland, Toys 'Я' Us or any such entertainment destinations. They didn't exist.

Our big day was Saturday when we were given a nickel to see a movie at the Bijou Theatre. After we were bathed and neatly dressed, we'd sit on the front steps with a clean handkerchief and a nickel waiting for the time to go. My brother, Red, was the one who took Trudy (who is two years older than I) and me to the movies.

Because there was no TV when I was growing up, the Bijou as entertainment was to us what TV, DVDs, computer games, and CDs are to today's generation. When we were at home, our only entertainment was the radio. The whole family would gather around the woodstove in the kitchen and listen to programs like *Inner Sanctum*, *We the People*, and *Mr. District Attorney*. No one talked; we sat there in silence and listened attentively while our imaginations visualized the scenes that were being enacted.

At the Bijou, we watched pictures of fun lifestyles with luxuries that come with achievement and success. I remember seeing silk sheets and beautiful lingerie in those black-and-white B movies and thinking, "One day I'll be rich and successful and I'll have silk sheets, too." Those images gave us hope and dreams of better things to come. We would talk among ourselves on the way home about our goals and dreams for the future.

Still, at the time, my brothers and sisters and I felt blessed when my dad took us twice a year to buy new clothes. We girls got a new outfit at Easter, and three dresses and one pair of shoes if we needed them at the beginning of each school year. We got one gift at Christmas—and we cherished it. We made our own ornaments for our Christmas tree with simple things like popcorn, paper link chains, and colored eggshells, the contents of which had been sucked out by my mother.

My favorite gift one year was a pair of roller skates. They were the kind you adjust with a skate key that usually hung around my neck on a string. I had them for years because as my foot grew, I could adjust the size. I can still recall learning to roller-skate. I was so thin that the skates felt like they weighed 50 pounds. When I finally got used to the feeling, roller-skating became my favorite thing to do. I remember thinking, "This is the closest thing to flying through the air."

I always wished for a bike, but throughout my whole childhood, I never owned one. The main reason was my dad's fear that we would get hurt, or worse, killed. He had almost killed a kid on a bike one day when he was on his way home. The boy had darted out in front of his car so fast that he couldn't keep from hitting the boy. Thankfully, the boy wasn't seriously hurt, but the incident left an indelible memory. Bobby, my oldest brother, was my only sibling lucky enough to have a bike. The reason he was singled out was because he was able to get a job delivering prescriptions for the local drugstore. The job required the delivery boy to have a bike, so my dad relented, first because the extra income would help, and second, he believed that every man (boy) should learn to be a provider.

When I was about five, I begged my brother to give me a ride on his bike. Reluctantly, he agreed to do so. It was close to Easter

Sunday so I had on my new, cute little red sandals. I was sitting on the handlebars and when Bobby made a turn, my foot got caught in the spokes of the bike. I screamed and I think my brother turned white as a sheet. My shoe was all mangled and I was crying (more because of my new shoes than from any pain). We were both afraid to go home. Luckily, Daddy wasn't home when we got there. As she often did, Mama covered for us, and I don't think he ever found out. His knowing about it would have further ensured that a bike was not in my future. Actually, his concerns turned out to be well-founded. One day while delivering prescriptions, my brother was hit by a car. He suffered a skull fracture, but he recovered rather quickly. That incident cemented a bikeless future for the rest of us kids.

It was around my freshman year in high school that, after 35 years of marriage, my parents divorced. I was the only one of their children who hadn't married, and my mother and I lived together next door to my older sister Elsie. I guess like most children of divorced parents, I never quite understood why my parents decided to call it quits after so many years. I know they loved each other because in later years Daddy told me that, even though he had remarried, he never loved anyone as much as my mother.

When my mother was very sick and the doctor kept telling us she would not last, she would suddenly rally again. This went on for over a month and finally her doctor asked, "Is there someone she's waiting to see?" The only person we could think of was Daddy. He was living in Texas, so I called him and asked him to come see her. Two days later he was there. When he went into her room, we all walked out so that they could be alone. For about 20 minutes, whatever they talked about—those were the last words Mama spoke. She went into a coma shortly after he left and died the next morning. So I have to believe that she loved him till the end and perhaps she wanted to tell him that.

Mama had been a beautiful redhead with brown eyes. Her skin was like porcelain, without a mark on it. She never went out into the sun. She would wear a hat and cover her face with a scarf when she hung out the laundry. When I'd come home sunburned in my efforts to achieve a tan, she'd ask, "Why would you want to punish your body like that?" It was beyond her comprehension that someone would deliberately expose themselves to the sun when she did everything she could to avoid it. She must have been a real beauty when she was young. It was painful to see her in her last days as her hair suddenly turned gray and she became rail thin, her cheeks sunken.

She married Daddy when she was 17 years old. He was a tall, handsome brunette. Actually he was only six feet, but that was considered tall at the time. He had a wonderful zest for life. His eyes were grayish green with the twinkle of a rogue. Everyone liked him immediately. He was the kind of guy who would walk into a bar and if he saw someone he knew he'd immediately send over a drink, even in hard times. He was always generous with his money and his love. He never passed up an opportunity to help a friend, and throughout his life he helped many. Daddy died in 1985 at the age of 86.

Some people say that children today don't get the same quality education as did the students of the so-called "great generation." I have often wondered: If it *is* true, then is it because of all the outside distractions? We had much more time to study and it was easier to focus, because there were not a lot of other things to think about. Back then, the consequences for not complying with the rules were far greater from the teachers and from the parents. Today, teachers are so constrained with dos and don'ts that they're afraid to discipline a student.

I am thankful for the discipline I received during my school years, even if I didn't like it at the time. After interviewing hundreds of applicants for job positions, I have found that many people who have college diplomas can't read and write. Their misspelled words, poor grammar, and illegible penmanship confirm that there are some graduates who didn't *earn* that piece of paper. Incoherent answers to written questions lead me to believe that they didn't learn how to read, either. How sad for them that they will be deprived of one of the greatest joys and bountiful pleasures in life.

I believe one of the reasons ours has been called "the great generation" is that we all learned at an early age that responsibility, hard work, and sacrifice were not an option, but an accepted obligation if we wanted to live in a free society.

Many teachers also underestimate the value of praise. I remember one day my second-grade teacher, Miss Honold, was going to mount a pencil sharpener inside a cabinet. Just as she was about to screw it down, I pointed out that there wasn't enough room for the pencil to fit—apparently she had considered only the space needed for the sharpener, forgetting that the pencil would need room, too. She smiled and said, "You're absolutely right. What a smart girl you are." She patted me on the head, and then announced to the class that I had saved her from making a mistake. I remember feeling embarrassed at the time, but I also felt important. Isn't it interesting that after 60 plus years I still remember that seemingly insignificant event? Oh, the power of praise!

I always liked school. I was a good student because I enjoyed learning new things. Even to this day, I enjoy reading about what's happening all over the world. I enjoy learning a new language or traveling to places I've read about. I hope I never lose my curiosity to discover new things. I sometimes worry that the children today have so much "stuff" that they take everything for granted and goal setting is a foreign exercise to them. With all the virtual reality and cyberspace activity, I worry that children aren't getting enough human interaction. We learn a lot from interaction with people and from watching the behavior of others in real-life situations. It is important in preparing us to be active participants in society.

Later in life and many years after I finished high school, I did take college courses at night in nutrition and management, and at different times classes in anthropology and French. I took them only for audit, at the University of Chicago, in the early 1970s. Because of my demanding work schedule, I had to drop them. I was working such long hours. I took these courses because I've always believed in education for education's sake; I don't believe that education has anything to do with success in business, and history has proven that time and again: Many people who have been really successful didn't complete their formal education.

Moreover, throughout my whole life, I have always educated myself. During my entire career, whenever I could read a book that I thought would enhance my understanding of the industry or business, I would buy it and read it.

A Waif of a Child

My sisters and brothers and I all had nicknames for each other. We called my oldest sister, Verna, "Freckles" whenever we wanted to annoy her, because she was self-conscious about her freckles. Our teasing certainly didn't help her to accept them. Elsie, my second oldest sister, was "Cora," after a very unattractive woman we knew. When we wanted to tease her, we'd call her Cora because Elsie was so beautiful; it was the ultimate insult. When we wanted to tease Red, we would call him "Marie Goog" after a crazy woman we knew. That would really upset him, making us feel that our goal was accomplished.

Trudy's nickname was the worst, though, because we sometimes called her "Fatso." She was on the plump side and Mama had to buy her clothes in a "chubby" size. Somehow Bobby escaped uncomplimentary nicknames, and my nickname was "Fenon," a French word whose meaning is not quite clear. In spite of the teasing and name calling, we all loved each other and we remained close until long after we all married and even after some of us moved away. In fact, I worked with two of my sisters, Trudy and Elsie, in several businesses.

In contrast to Trudy, I was teased unmercifully about my frail body. I was a waif of a child. My dad would prepare a drink of milk, raw eggs, vanilla, and who knows what else for me every day. It's a wonder I didn't grow up to be a hypochondriac because Mama often said, "I know that child must have TB—she's too thin." Actually, I was very healthy. Perhaps the daily dose of cod liver oil helped, but I don't think I even had frequent colds. Cod liver oil is very unpleasant, but I got so used to taking it that I would actually remind my mother when it was time for my daily dose. I guess the saying "You can even get used to hanging by your thumbs if you hang *long* enough" is true.

Being so thin had other disadvantages. Because Trudy was a chubby kid, she needed to get new shoes more often than me. Due to her excess weight, her shoes would wear out much faster. On the other hand, mine seemed to never wear out. I remember returning home from school after a rain, walking the whole distance in the gutter where the rain had collected, so I would ruin my shoes enough to warrant new ones. I don't think I ever wore out a pair of shoes. The only time I got new school shoes was when my feet were too large for the old ones or at the start of each school year.

We were well fed as children, too, but we ate healthy meals, though my mama did cook with butter. That was the norm back then—nobody knew then what effect butter had on your cholesterol. We didn't even know the word *cholesterol* at the time! But we always ate fresh foods. My mama's whole life was her family: She cooked three meals a day and left the house only to walk to the corner grocery store when we weren't available to do it for her. She had a vegetable garden and she raised chickens. Her meals often consisted of different ways of preparing chicken and fresh vegetables. I can still see her wringing the chicken's neck while explaining to us that it was the most painless and humane way to kill a chicken for cooking. Mama was so gentle, we knew she wouldn't do anything to hurt an animal. She tried to avoid having us see her do her "dirty work," but sometimes it was unavoidable, so she did her best to explain why it was necessary.

One Easter, we were given baby ducklings that became pets. As they grew, they would try to fly over our fence. One day, they disappeared and caused us to wonder did they really fly away as Mama said, or were they one of the tasty meals she usually prepared? I really didn't want to know.

Every morning as children, we had oatmeal for breakfast. Some days, we would be sitting and eating our oatmeal while Mama ate scrambled eggs with calf brains, which caused me to feel like gagging. That's a delicacy I still cannot convince myself to enjoy. But she loved it!

Mama insisted that we come home from school for lunch. I don't know if that was because she didn't think school meals were nutritious or fresh enough or because of the added cost. In any case, we came home to freshly made vegetable or chicken soup along with peanut butter and jelly sandwiches made with fresh-baked bread.

We lived 12 blocks from school, so we had to walk 12 blocks in the morning, 24 back and forth for lunch, then 12 to come home at the end of the school day (48 blocks total) each day. It's no wonder I was so skinny. One thing I'm sure of: Walking is an excellent exercise. It is still my personal favorite method of exercise.

Recalling my teenage years, I am reminded of how timing can make such a difference in any outcome as well as in one's perception of things. Back then, I had what today would be described as an ideal figure, trim and well-proportioned. However, I felt I was painfully thin and longed to have a more curvaceous body, which was the ideal at that time. When purchasing skirts or pants, the smallest waistline size available was 22 inches. I remember having to take in all the waistlines, so although I never measured my waist, I know it was smaller than 22 inches. It wasn't until Twiggy came on the scene that "thin was in." After Twiggy changed the standard, I longed to have that waistline again. From then on I thought, "Where was Twiggy when I needed her?"

For a brief time during high school, I worked for Godchaux's, a local high-end department store that catered to the elite. I was asked to model their clothes for the store's fashion shows. I've always been somewhat of a clotheshorse, so I jumped at the chance. Another "first" happened to me while I worked for Godchaux's. The powers that be urged me to enter the Miss Godchaux beauty pageant. Reluctantly I did so, and to my surprise I won the title. I think that was the first time I considered that possibly I wasn't too skinny after all.

I was then offered a modeling contract with the lingerie company Vanity Fair, but I declined the offer because I was planning to leave New Orleans with my sister Elsie. It's funny how one decision, one right turn instead of a left one, can change your whole life's course. If I had remained in New Orleans and/or taken that offer, my life would probably have gone in an entirely different direction. Perhaps the good thing about that is I will never know how life might have turned out otherwise!

It's funny how one decision,
one right turn instead of a left one,
can change your whole life's course.

21

2

First Foray into Entrepreneurship

"You can do anything and be anything you want."

After high school, I went to Miami, Florida, with my sister Elsie. She had secretly eloped when she was 15 years old, and she was now divorcing her husband and going to Miami for a singing job. She asked me to go with her so I could help care for her son, Billy. That began quite an adventure. In Miami, she worked for a Greek guy named Ernie, who owned a nightclub there, and we had a lot of fun times. But after a year and a half, I missed New Orleans and I missed my family, whom I hadn't seen since I left for Miami. So I went to visit for Christmas, 1952.

That trip to New Orleans changed my whole life. I was staying with my brother Bobby and his wife Mabel, and they introduced me to their next-door neighbor Robert Bourcq, also called Bobby. He was a handsome young man who had achieved quite a record in powerboat racing. In fact, he is in the Hall of Fame with speed records that still have never been broken. He was charming and cute. He was also a fishing and hunting buddy to my brother, so they saw quite a lot of each other. While I was staying next door to him, Bobby B. came over often. I could tell he liked me, but he didn't ask me out.

While I was visiting, I was offered a job with a prominent oral surgeon (Dr. Fontenot), so I accepted and decided to remain in New Orleans. I assisted in surgery, because I had previous experience working in the dental clinic of Charity Hospital during the summers when I was in high school. I had enjoyed the work and at one time had considered becoming a dental hygienist. During my time at the hospital, the chief of oral surgery had suggested I go into the dentistry field because he felt I had a natural ability.

One reason I didn't pursue it, though, was because there was no school program in New Orleans then, and I couldn't leave New Orleans because my mother was quite ill at the time. I was the only sibling who was unmarried, so I had to take a big part of the responsibility for her care.

Mama had three strokes and eventually her kidneys stopped functioning and she passed away in 1951. That was a very traumatic time for me. Prior to her death, she was hospitalized for almost three months and I stayed with her from early morning until late evening.

The Beginning of a New Relationship

During the same time period that I went to work for Dr. Fontenot, my sister Trudy and her husband Guido were going through a divorce. She decided to move back to New Orleans with her two daughters, Cathy and Debbie. We rented a house together that was not far from Bobby and Mabel. I would often drop by their house after work for a cup of coffee and a chat.

On one such occasion, Bobby Bourcq was there. When it was time for me to leave, he asked me if he could drive me home, because I didn't have a car. My transportation in those days was city buses. I said yes and when we got to my house, he asked me for a date. Whether he was shy or just afraid of rejection, I was tickled by how long it had taken him to get the courage to do so. I accepted the invitation and that was the beginning of our relationship.

I thought Bobby was cute, but I didn't see him as the one I would marry. I think Mabel had a lot to do with changing my mind about that. She said to me one day, "Don't get too serious about Bobby Bourcq. He's a confirmed bachelor, and your relationship will go nowhere." I think deep down Mabel had a crush on him, and even though she was married, she didn't want to see him taken away. In any case, it became a challenge to prove her wrong. I have never been one to readily accept the words, "You *can't* do it."

I have never been one to readily accept the words, "You *can't* do it."

After dating for a year, Bobby asked me to marry him, and I accepted. We were married in a little church by Father Higgenbothom, a Catholic priest, on August 7, 1954, my 22nd birthday. It was a lovely wedding. I wore a three-quarter-length French lace gown, which was very "in" at the time. We rode to our honeymoon in Biloxi, Mississippi, in a new red convertible Cadillac, which belonged to my sister Trudy's new boyfriend, Calvin, whom she later married.

On June 5, 1955, our daughter, Denise Patricia, was born. She weighed six pounds, three ounces. She was a beautiful baby. Her head remained hairless until she was about one year old. Then the corkscrew curls popped out, and her head became a mass of ringlets. When I took her shopping with me, I remember people stopping me to say how beautiful she was. She was a good baby, too. She never cried as an infant.

In fact, before I took Denise home from the hospital, I told the nurse that she had not cried anytime during my one-week stay (one week being customary in those days). With a thumb and middle finger the nurse snapped her on the bottom of her foot and Denise let out a yell and began to cry. I knew then that she was okay, and I was so thankful that she was normal but just content. We were a happy family.

After a year or so, Bobby and I wanted to have another baby. We stopped practicing birth control but I couldn't seem to get pregnant. Three years went by after Denise's birth and we decided it was not meant to be. But we were wrong: Michelle Rae was born on April 1, 1959, almost four years after Denise.

Michelle was the opposite of Denise. She cried often and wouldn't allow me a night's sleep. I tried to nurse her, but she was hungry all the time. I figured my milk was not rich or satisfying enough for her, so I switched to prepared formulas. She always seemed to be starving, so at six weeks I began putting a little pablum (cereal) in her formula and she loved it. The first day I gave it to her she slept soundly that night and I was able to get my first full night's rest.

Since Michelle's infancy, I have been a proponent for giving infants a small amount of solids at an early age. I know that flies in the face of conventional wisdom, but Michelle is living proof that it does no harm as she grew up a healthy child and today she is an active, energetic, and healthy adult. Aside from the common cold, she has been free of any illness thus far in 43 years.

Michelle has always delighted me no end. As a darling baby she was always smiling. As a child she would say the most humorous things, and she took forever to tell a story giving vivid descriptions of every detail.

She also managed to do things in an unconventional way that seemed to sometimes get her into trouble. At work, people would often ask me, "What did Michelle do today?" They seemed to enjoy her antics as much as we did. For instance, Michelle rode her horse to the picnic grounds for a school picnic, and the horse proceeded to empty his bowels right where everyone was planning to eat. Mother Superior sent her home along with her horse; however, instead of going directly home, Michelle dismounted and entered a relay race. For disobeying, she was suspended from school for three days. Listening to Michelle tell the story was a trip in itself. God is just and he has given Michelle a daughter with many of the same endearing attributes that continue to amuse and remind me of Michelle in her early years.

Working to Supplement Our Family Income

During my pregnancy with Denise, I continued to work as a dental assistant until two weeks before she was born. After her birth, I felt that nine-hour workdays would take me away from her too much, so I began to look around for another kind of job that would help to supplement our family income.

I responded to an ad in the *Times-Picayune* for outside sales. It was for a job selling china, silver, and crystal to prospective brides. What attracted me to this ad was that the hours were flexible; it wasn't a full-time commitment. There are limited types of work one can do outside the home that don't require you to go to an office and spend a specified amount of time, and most of what was available at that time were sales jobs. I'm not so sure that it would be as lucrative a business today, with rising gas prices and traffic delays.

And even though I had no sales experience, for as long as I can remember I've felt that I could do anything. My dad always told me "You can *do* anything and *be* anything you want, if you want it bad enough." Thank goodness, he didn't tell me I could fly, because I probably would have tried that, too! But I was never afraid of failure; call it confidence, call it cockiness—I was never afraid to try anything.

I immediately liked Coralie Regas, the woman who interviewed me. She was the head honcho in Louisiana for Home Decorators. She was the zone manager, which was a person who maintained $10,000 per month in sales. She was looking for people to work in her zone.

For as long as I can remember
I've felt that I could do anything.

My best friend, Anita Landry, came along on the interview, because she was also looking for part-time work. She was pregnant at the time, and her husband was a law student. Anita has been one of my lifelong friends; I've known her as long as I can remember. Anita lived in my neighborhood. She is a little older than I so we weren't classmates. I met her in my early twenties, and she became a trusted friend who took Denise into her home while I was in the hospital for the birth of Michelle. Our children grew up together and her son Nicky was like the son I never had.

Anita and her relatives always treated my children and me like members of their own family. During our time here on earth, few people enter one's life and form the kind of friendship bonds that link them together for life. They are people who can communicate their support without having to use words, knowing how you feel, then only saying what needs to be said. Anita is that kind of person to me. Even though we live many miles apart, I continue to think of her often and with affection. I still revisit the vivid memories of the fun times we had together.

Fortunately, Coralie hired us both, and we joined the Home Decorators company, which was a branch of International Silver. I think Coralie hired me because of my enthusiasm, but also because of the way I looked: I was attractive, well-dressed—you know, all the reasons you hire anyone—a gut feeling, I guess.

27

That was the beginning of my career in sales. I learned so much about selling, but most of all I learned a lot about people and what motivates their purchases. For example, I often talked to the single girls I called on about the importance of homemaking and how rewarding it is. I emphasized how much fun it is when you're looking forward to being a bride and spending time in your new home, making your home a place that you're proud to invite your friends to. I created an image of what appeals to a girl that age, at that time.

And it helped a lot, when I was at Home Decorators, that I was close to the same age as my customers. In fact, I looked much younger than I was. I was often asked by the parents of the girls I was calling on, "Did you go to school with my daughter?" That always tickled me, because I was in my twenties, calling on girls who had just graduated from high school.

As I mentioned, the company's products were china, silver, and crystal that were sold to prospective brides. Sales reps needed to know who was getting married, who was going to college, and who was going to go to work. Our sales technique was to get a list of graduating students from local high schools; then we would contact one girl on the list, and we hoped that person would tell us which of her friends were getting married. Usually, the first girl we contacted would give us all the information about her friends in the graduating class, so we had an "in" as soon as we went to the homes of the girls she recommended. We could say, "Mary Smith asked me to stop by to see you," so we were immediately welcomed into the home. It was basically door-to-door sales, but we weren't cold-calling, because we set up our visits in advance from recommendations: We would call and say we're coming by, or we'd set up an appointment. Sometimes we would just drop in, for example, if a girl recommended someone who was a close neighbor of hers. We might just stop by and see if she was home and make the sales call right then and there.

During the week I worked in the evenings when Bobby was home to take care of Denise. Bobby would get home at five o'clock, so I could call on two or three people in an evening. But most of my sales were made on Saturdays. I often made as many as six sales on one Saturday. Bobby and I still had time together, because I never worked past nine o'clock at night, and we spent Sundays together. My situation wasn't very different from most working women at that time: There were women working outside the home—but there weren't many women-owned businesses. Of course, I didn't run my own business until much later in my life.

I don't think Bobby was *thrilled* that I was working, but he wasn't unhappy, either. He recognized that the added income that I brought into the home allowed us to do things that maybe we couldn't have done on his salary alone. For example, our daughters went to private school, we always took nice vacations, and the girls had nice clothes. Not that he couldn't have supplied those things on his own, but we couldn't have done as much as we did without the second income. I think he appreciated the added income, though if he had had a choice, he probably would have preferred that I was at home since some of the responsibility for taking care of the kids was on his shoulders, even after we hired a nanny.

My First Success in Sales

Soon, Anita was selling $10,000 a month, and I was selling $10,000 a month. This happened within the first three to six months, which was very fast. The Home Decorators division was divided into zones. Each zone was determined by the amount of business it produced; it had nothing to do with geography. One zone had to produce a minimum of $10,000 in sales a month to keep that status. Coralie was responsible for one zone. But when Anita and I each reached the $10,000 level, we really created two more zones within the zone because Coralie's zone was now producing $30,000 a month, which had never happened before in the company.

So I became a zone leader, which meant I had the responsibility to hire people for my zone, just as Coralie had done. Soon I had 12 people working for me. One of the first people I hired turned out to be a superstar, a real sales phenomenon: Her name was Lucille Foster. I'll never forget the interview. She arrived at my home with her husband, who sat out in their car. I invited her to ask him in, and she told me he was a paraplegic who had lost the use of his legs in a car accident and he preferred to remain in the car. I explained what would be expected of her, but she replied, "I don't think I could sell anything." How wrong she was!

After I explained that selling is nothing more than communicating a solution that fulfills a need, Lucille came aboard. She was a lovely young girl, with these big beautiful eyes, and she was so convincing because she looked so innocent, so everyone she talked to bought from her. In her first month, she became the single highest producer in my zone. She was to become one of my best friends and remained so for many years after I left Home Decorators.

The time I spent with Home Decorators was fun for me because we were the most successful area in the country. Anita and I won a trip to International Silver headquarters in Newark, New York, where we were given tours of the plants and attended an awards banquet. We met all kinds of interesting people there, and I couldn't wait for our Monday night meeting back home to tell everyone of our exciting experiences. One of the people we met was a sergeant in the army. He had us doubling up with laughter as he recounted his presentation and how he convinced the men to work for him selling the products in their free evenings! Being granted weekend furloughs as their reward was a strong incentive for his recruits.

Every Monday we held a meeting at Coralie's home to recognize the superachievers and to train on giving presentations and closing sales. As we told of the fun and interesting time we had in

FIRST FORAY INTO ENTREPRENEURSHIP

Newark, I could see the excitement it engendered in all the other sales reps aspiring to be the best. I worked for Home Decorators for four years, all through my pregnancy with Michelle and part-time after she was born in 1959. I don't know if the company is still in business today, but I've been to swaps where I've seen patterns of the products we sold.

I found that I loved people.
I loved communicating with people—
hearing their stories, and
just talking to them.

The time I spent with that organization was a wonderful learning experience, and it was responsible for cherished friendships that have remained with me throughout the years. Also, I found that I loved people. I loved communicating with people—hearing their stories, and just talking to them. And when I could satisfy a need they might have, it gave me a good feeling of achievement and fulfillment.

A New Partnership

While I was still working for Home Decorators, Anita started her own business. She contacted a manufacturer of stainless steel cookware and found that for a minimum purchase of product, she could become a distributor. Stainless steel was becoming popular as a much healthier metal than other metals then used in cooking. She felt that the timing was good to introduce that product in much the same way we had sold the Home Decorators products, that is, door-to-door to prospective brides.

We had always worked well together as a team, so when she invited me to work with her, I happily did so. I wasn't a partner in the business in the real sense, but whatever we sold together, I got half the commission, which was a sizable amount in those days. So her business was profitable for us both.

I had always worked with a partner for evening calls because I didn't feel it was safe to go out alone at night. I'm sure there were times when due to circumstances beyond my control I had to do so reluctantly, but I tried to avoid it whenever possible. Besides the safety factor, having a friend along made the work more like a fun adventure.

Anita had taken what we had learned and the experience we got while working with Home Decorators and started a new business. She was able to solve the problem of lag time by keeping an inventory of cookware in a local warehouse making it available for immediate delivery.

Anita and I continued to offer the Home Decorator products while her new business was growing. There was no conflict of interest because Home Decorators did not offer cookware at that time and we were independent sales reps. Cookware was a new and exciting product for us to present, and we approached it with renewed enthusiasm. We felt we now had a complete line of essentials for entertaining in the home.

Usually a client would purchase one or two of the products—china and silverware, china and crystal, silverware and cookware, or any other combination. Once in a while we would sell three products to one client, and that was a home run. How much clients purchased depended greatly on their economic circumstances. We both worked very hard, but there were fun experiences, too. One such experience happened when we were traveling from one rural area to the next. We called on a prospect and as we were presenting our samples Anita, who was sitting opposite me on a couch, saw a mouse dancing around my feet under my chair. She knew I was deathly afraid of mice so she kept stomping her feet in an effort to scare the little critter away. Apparently it wasn't working because she kept using more and more force. I was raising my voice in an effort to drown out the noise coming from her stomping while giving her questioning looks. After we left the house she explained her dilemma and the reason for her loud choreography. We both cried with laughter as we envisioned the scene that would have ensued if that mouse had run over my foot or up my leg.

I continued to work with Anita whenever I could throughout my pregnancy with Michelle. That was not as often as I would have liked. I was often nauseated and experiencing nonstop vomiting so that I had to remain in bed. There were days when I just couldn't get up. My doctor had given me suppositories to alleviate the vomiting and they made me sleepy, and unsteady. So when I did feel well enough to work I welcomed the opportunity to take my mind off my discomfort.

My second pregnancy was so different from my first. For my first I was able to work until shortly before Denise was born. I remember the doctor I worked for saying, "Jenny, you are going to have to stop working or I'll be the one to deliver that baby." At full term I had gained only 16 pounds, so immediately after Denise was born I was wearing all my prepregnancy clothes again. By contrast, because I was nauseated most of the time during my pregnancy with Michelle, my doctor had advised me to eat soda crackers and ginger ale at 20-minute intervals. That worked for a while; then I began to eat peanut butter and jelly sandwiches, sometimes adding bananas. Slowly I increased the amounts and continued the frequency, since eating always made me feel better.

Well, you can imagine what happened: I gained 50 pounds during my pregnancy. Between eating all the wrong foods in greater quantity and not having enough activity to burn the extra calories it was easy to pack on the pounds. Sound familiar?

Michelle's birth was another turning point in my life and in my career. I figured, as with Denise, that all that fat was going to disappear quickly. Sadly, that didn't happen.

After three months, I was still more than 30 pounds overweight. When I looked in the mirror, I resembled my mother. I guess she was 30 pounds overweight, though she wasn't obese. I didn't think about her weight when I was growing up, because I was so skinny then, I wanted to have *more* weight. Skinny wasn't "in," because girls who were more curvaceous were more popular, and my measurements were probably 19-19-19. I looked like a stick figure.

I'm sure my mother's weight had something to do with her strokes, and consequently, her death. My dad was never overweight, but my mother's entire family was plump. She had nine brothers and sisters, eight of whom died before the age of 50. They all had high blood pressure, and they were all overweight. And now I was, too.

I decided to do something about it. I went to the local gym, Silhouette/American Health. At that time, a gym was the only recourse available for someone wanting to lose weight. I suppose Weight Watchers may have been around: I think it started in 1951, but I wasn't aware of it. The gym was the only thing I was aware of that could offer some degree of help.

The gym had weight machines but nothing as sophisticated as gyms of today have. We had old-fashioned leg press machines, bench press machines, and a "butterfly" machine that had a padded roller on each side. You would place your hands behind your neck and proceed to use your elbows to bring the bar up to a 90-degree angle. That was meant to work the pectoral muscles. We also had barrel rollers that performed a kneading effect on fatty areas of the body along with the vibrator belts that were designed to break down fatty tissue. If the people who attended the gyms back then were to walk into a modern gym with today's advanced mechanically designed equipment, surely they would think they were on another planet.

I began an exercise routine. I had already modified my diet, because it was not necessary to control nausea that no longer existed. I was once again eating healthfully and living an active lifestyle. I didn't have to change my diet completely; I simply cut down on what I was eating, reducing the portion size, trying not to eat so much. And I did avoid eating a lot of bread, potatoes, and starches.

The gym was co-ed, but it was segregated: women went Mondays, Wednesdays, and Fridays, and men went Tuesdays, Thursdays, and Saturdays. This schedule was intended to make men and women comfortable, just like single-sex gyms do today. Joining Silhouette was the beginning of my education in weight loss and how it affects one's self-image. As I attended the gym in the beginning, I noticed how most women who came there to work out didn't talk a lot. I've always been very outgoing, but I noticed that other women who came to the gym always had their heads down; they went about their business and they used the machines, but they didn't talk to anyone.

At first, I thought they just were introverted people, but then I noticed they seemed to be self-conscious and downhearted. As a woman at the gym lost weight, I saw her whole demeanor—as well as her personality—go through a change. Those same women started out rather plain and unhappy, but after they started losing weight and got toned up, they came in with new hairdos, they began to apply makeup, and they walked upright with a bounce to their steps. I was just *fascinated* at how someone's personality could change because of their appearance, and it made me realize that appearance has a lot to do with personality—how you project yourself, and how other people see you.

As a woman at the gym lost weight,
I saw her whole demeanor—
as well as her personality—
go through a change.

35

I'm certain that I came across that way to other people, too. Even though I'm normally a very outgoing person, without realizing it, I probably felt self-conscious about the way I looked. And then I was probably going through the same metamorphosis.

I was just *fascinated* at how someone's personality could change because of their appearance.

I began to research the whole topic of weight loss, because it was an experience I was unfamiliar with, having been thin for most of my life. It's surprising how little there was available back then. First, I went to the library, only to find that all that was available were textbooks, which I found boring and certainly not what I was looking for. There wasn't much written in layman's terms to explain the whole concept of why we gain weight and what influence it has on us.

So I went to the bookstores, and there wasn't much available there, either. Today, there are huge sections of how-to books on diet, nutrition, and exercise. But in 1959, the only books I could find were three by Adele Davis, and they were available only in health-food stores! Adele Davis was a pioneer on the subject of health and the role food plays in our overall well-being. She may not have been the first, but she was certainly one of the first to bring this link to the public's attention.

Combining My Sales Experience with My Personal Experience

It took me about three months to lose the 30 pounds left over after Michelle was born. And after I lost most of my weight, the gym manager offered me a job selling memberships and teaching members how to use the machines. He was impressed because I had been coming regularly and had lost so much weight; I also knew many of the members. Similarly, many Jenny Craig counselors today are former clients. They can give a personal testimonial: "I've been through it; I know what you're going through, and here's how *I* handled it." Clients are a built-in resource for recruiting employees because of their commitment and dedication. Perhaps the Silhouette manager saw that in me, as well as my enthusiasm.

I accepted the job primarily because I was hooked on the topic of weight loss and self-image, but also because the job only required that I work part-time: Mondays, Wednesdays, and Fridays. It was a lot of hours, though: I worked 12 hours on each of those three days. Still, working only three days a week meant I could spend more time with my two girls. My hours were 9 A.M. to 9 P.M.

By this time, Bobby and I had hired a live-in nanny to help take care of the girls while both of us were at work. Still, on the days I worked, I got up early and cooked dinner for the family, because my children couldn't wait to eat as late as I got home. I would cook things like casseroles and roast chicken or meatloaf, things that could be easily heated when Bobby got home from work. He didn't know the first thing about cooking then, and there were no microwaves and few other conveniences at that time. And I have always enjoyed cooking.

Even now that I no longer have to cook a lot, whenever I feel stressed or concerned about something, I head to the kitchen and start cooking. I will cook several different meals at one time and take them to one of my daughters for her family to eat. Or, if I cook several different kinds of soup, I will freeze meal-size portions for future quick meals.

Adele Digby and Lucille Foster, two of my good friends from our Home Decorators days, had both come to work at Silhouette. We were quite a team. Compared to the other centers in the chain, our center was always on top in terms of the number of customers, which meant in terms of revenue as well. We all loved the work, and we were dedicated to making all the members successful. Adele and Lucille did the same thing I was doing: selling memberships and assisting clients by showing them how to use the equipment.

It was almost like co-managing, though, because we all collected the money, made the deposits, and did the bookkeeping. We were also very competitive, not with each other, but with other gyms within the chain of company-owned locations. We had so much fun at work that I couldn't wait to get back to the gym after my days off.

The company often held contests among the four gyms in New Orleans. During one such contest when we had worked really hard to win, the owners refused to name us as winners because deep down I think they wanted another team to win. They made the excuse that they needed to verify the figures before they could declare the winners.

Three weeks passed, and they still hadn't done so. Our members were up in arms because they had all worked hard bringing in guests who by enrolling in the program would help us win. Finally, after almost a month had passed since the end of the contest, we were declared the winners. It was a bittersweet victory, though. This incident taught me a lot about the art of motivation and the importance of fairness.

I continued to work for Silhouette for about five years, in a variety of locations throughout the greater New Orleans area.

Earlier, Silhouette/American Health had been a public company. Sometime after I started to work there, the company had gone private and the senior executives had closed some gyms and split up those that remained. The people for whom I worked owned the New Orleans gyms along with gyms in Corpus Christi, Texas, as their piece of the breakup. During the years I worked for my new bosses, I realized that they were a little different in their approach with personnel. In addition to the kind of treatment we received in the unfair contest incident, during many of the meetings that were held—instead of praising employees for a job well done—they pointed out publicly all the things we were doing wrong or not doing at all. For instance, in the corner of the room where meetings were held there was a high stool. They would single out an employee who had trouble collecting money from the members, place a dunce cap on his/her head, give them a wallpaper brush (signifying that they could only write, not collect money), and have them sit on the stool throughout the meeting. While working there I learned many valuable lessons that have guided me throughout the years of owning my own companies, one of which is to always *praise in public, scold in private.* (However, I must point out that personally I was never a victim of this chastising.) There were other things I thought important that were being ignored, so I began to think about changing jobs or going into business for myself.

My First Venture into Entrepreneurship

Soon after that I decided to open my own business. I wanted to be my own boss, and working in a gym was the only experience I had, other than working in a dental office and selling products for Home Decorators. I didn't want to go back to selling door-to-door with Home Decorators as I was ready to move on.

> I wanted to be my own boss,
> and working in a gym
> was the only experience I had.

I discussed the idea of opening a gym with my friend and coworker, Adele Digby. She and I felt that if we were calling the shots we could add a lot to what was being offered in other gyms throughout the city. After deciding it was a great opportunity, we began to look around to see what locations were available and what our investment would have to be. It wasn't long before we discovered a good location where the landlord was willing to give us a building allowance for the renovations that would be amortized over the period of the lease. Since Bobby was a builder, he was able to save us quite a lot of money by doing the construction work necessary prior to opening.

Our greatest expense was the purchase of all the equipment. Both Adele and I had some savings available but we knew that we would need cash for an advertising campaign and start-up costs that are part of doing business. We also planned to have a cash reserve in case things didn't go as well as we had expected. I knew, too, that our home was available to mortgage since it was almost debt free. Most of the homes we lived in Bobby had built. In most cases we had only small mortgages or none at all because we realized a good profit from the sale of each house and we parlayed that into the next. Bobby agreed that if it was necessary we could mortgage the house we were living in as long as the business showed some promise.

I have been asked why I chose Adele as a business partner rather than Bobby. The answer is simple: He wasn't the least bit interested in our field of work other than to lend his support, in much the same way I was not interested in joining him in his business of building homes and fences except to offer help and support when requested.

Starting my own business was exciting. It was work I knew and understood, and there was the added excitement of starting a business from scratch myself. Another benefit was that I truly enjoyed the work.

We pondered what to name our new business, and after tossing around some options we decided on Healthletic, a gym for both men and women. We thought it was a unisex name, neither feminine nor masculine, that would send a message that excercise was

40

physical and healthy, too. From the first day our new venture was showing promise.

One reason our business was profitable early on was that we got support from the bank that Bobby and I had always done business with. Metairie Bank agreed to finance our members' program when members couldn't pay the full amount up front themselves. Immediately after a member enrolled, we received from Metairie Bank the full amount of the contract for each such program. Third-party transactions were not uncommon in those days, but most of the gyms did business with finance companies. In those days finance companies were allowed to charge a high interest rate, thus making doing business with them a last resort; many people were reluctant to get involved with them. By contrast, Metairie Bank financed our memberships at the going rate of bank loans.

To my knowledge, this was the first time Metairie Bank had financed a membership contract. Perhaps the reason the bankers agreed to do so was that Bobby and I had done business with them for many years and we had several accounts with them. A couple of the officers also knew Adele and thought that anything we were involved in would be legitimate and have a good chance for success. It was good to have the creditability of the bank along with the lower interest rates that made our members' monthly payments to the bank lower than they would have been had they gone through a finance company.

Adele and I knew the mayor who came to cut the ribbon for our grand opening. It was an exciting day, and it was fun to see our picture and read all about our new business in the paper the next day. I guess in some ways it's like your first car, first kiss, first girl/boyfriend: You never forget the feeling. Pride of ownership is powerful!

It was a new, good, and exciting experience designing our own advertising. Having to design and place the ads was good training that would become a valuable skill later on in my career. While Adele and I both had experience in sales, this was our first introduction to the power of marketing. We made mistakes, but eventually we learned a lot about how to make the phone ring for the least amount of money. Cost per lead is a critical component in any immediate response advertising.

Even though our gym was 3,000 square feet and relatively small by today's standards, it was typical of gyms in the area at that time. We could accommodate about 20 people working out at one time in contrast to 100 or more, which is not uncommon to see in gyms of today.

I have been asked about what business plan we started with. We didn't have a formal business plan; we simply knew what we needed to do to become profitable and we did it. However, that doesn't mean that we didn't have financial goals. Our short-term goal was to increase our gross sales by 10 percent each month. Even though that was an aggressive goal, I have learned that it's better to shoot for the moon and hit a star than it is to shoot for a tree and hit a rock. Our break-even point was in the area of $30,000 each month. Each client paid monthly dues in addition to an enrollment fee that was paid up front. We knew that eventually the dues from all the members would cover our expenses. That being so meant that revenue from all new enrollments would drop to the bottom line.

> We didn't have a formal business plan;
> we simply knew what we needed to do
> to become profitable and we did it.

We operated Healthletic successfully for a couple of years. Then our old bosses from Silhouette came to us to buy us out. Apparently they had been tracking our success even to the point of having someone sit outside our gym in a car counting the number of people going in and out each day. Our first response to them was, "No, thank you, we're not interested in selling our business now." They persisted, saying that they would open a larger and more luxurious spa down the block from us on a very busy intersection. Our attorney contacted them to ask why they were so anxious to acquire our gym since they had several in the area already. He told us their answer was, "We're most interested in acquiring the management team."

Our attorney urged us to sell to them, because he felt they would make good their promise to open a gym close to us, which would have hurt our business, as people would see their sign first on the way to our gym. They would also have the exposure on a well-traveled street, contrary to our location on a side street.

To make a long story short, we agreed to sell to them and we signed a one-year management contract. One thing I knew was that I wanted to be self-employed. I didn't like working for inflexible people who wouldn't consider my suggestions. So I knew that as soon as my management contract was up, I would look for another business to own.

3

Researching New Franchise Opportunities

"I was open to anything that was available."

During the year I was working for my former bosses at Silhouette, my sister Elsie and Muriel Boudreaux, a friend of ours who had also worked in the gym business (including Silhouette), heard about a new method of inch loss that involved wrapping people with gauze-like cloths soaked in a special solution. Actually, the technique was used by monks in monasteries centuries ago, but this method was considered to be the latest fad. All the process really did was force fluids from the areas that were wrapped, thus reducing them. However, after liquids were drunk, the inches gradually came back. Still, the temporary reduction served a purpose, especially if you had an important event that day and your favorite dress was too tight.

Elsie and Muriel contacted the company that introduced the method, and they were able to secure a franchise for the greater New Orleans area. The president of that company was Sid Craig. He sold them the franchise with the stipulation that they would buy the solution from him. However, the solution was not a patented formula.

Once they bought the franchise, though, Elsie and Muriel had the solution chemically analyzed. They found that they could produce it for considerably less money than what it cost them to buy it from Sid—almost one-fourth of what he was selling it to them for—so they stopped buying it from Sid. Naturally, this created some friction between Sid and Elsie, and they ended up on bad terms.

Meanwhile, my management contract ended, and about several months after Elsie and Muriel had started up their own business Elsie called me to say they were very busy. Could I work for a while to help them out? I agreed to help them while I looked around for a new franchise of my own. I did for Elsie and Muriel what I'd done for my own business (in other words, everything!): I answered the phones, scheduled appointments, sold series of wraps to customers, and helped with the bookkeeping. I guess I didn't really do *everything*, though, because I don't think I ever helped to wrap anyone in the gauze with the special solution!

Elsie and Muriel had named their business Slim Figures, and I remember answering the phone one day, "Slim Figures, may I help you?" and this very masculine voice answered, "Hi, Slim!" I burst out laughing because we rarely got calls from men, and I had never been called "Slim" by a caller. I soon learned that the caller was Sid Craig. We had never met; I had only heard about him from Elsie. Little did I know that I would soon meet him in person.

Working for Slim Figures was only temporary for me, though; I was just helping out my sister and friend. Every day I would scan the newspaper for opportunities. I didn't want to open another gym; that wouldn't make sense. Adele and I had sold ours, so I didn't want to go through the expense of opening another, and I thought we would get sued if I tried to open another gym close to where our former gym was. Other than a gym, I was open to anything that was available.

Because I went into the weight-management business at such a young age—I was not yet 28 years old—and because I was so fascinated and captivated by it, I don't think I considered doing anything else at that time. And then once I had my own business, the only other business I ever considered was a cosmetics franchise, and that was because I was interested in having a franchise more than I was interested in changing careers. There weren't a lot of franchises available other than fast-food franchises, which I didn't want to do because of my belief in the importance of a good, healthy, balanced diet.

One day I saw an ad explaining a new method of figure control that was soon to be introduced in the area. The first thing that came to mind was the possible opportunity for a franchise. So I decided to check it out. I called for information, only to find out that the president of that company was none other than Mr. Sid Craig! I made an appointment for an interview, not mentioning that I was Elsie's sister. This was easy to disguise, because our married names were different: Elsie's last name was Dolin, and mine was Bourcq. As I mentioned, Sid and Elsie had had a falling out and had parted ways in unfriendly circumstances. I knew he would not be too receptive to her sister asking for a franchise of his new company.

When I entered the lobby of the building where I was to be interviewed, to my surprise my sister Trudy was sitting there. Neither of us had indicated to the other that we planned to be there. Trudy was working for Silhouette, just down the street from where the interviews were being conducted, so she went on her lunch hour to check it out and see what it was, just as I was doing. She also hadn't mentioned that Elsie was her sister, because she also knew Sid still wasn't happy about the breakup of his and Elsie's business relationship. Trudy's last name was LeCompte, so Sid wouldn't have recognized her name. And neither of us looked enough like Elsie that he would know we were sisters: Trudy and I were both brunettes with brown eyes, and Elsie is a green-eyed redhead.

After a few minutes, this handsome guy came out into the lobby. He walked over to me and said, "Hi, you must be Alice." (That's what we'll call her.) He thought I was the trainer that his partner had sent him from Gloria Marshall headquarters in California. He had never seen her, so he didn't know what to expect. I assured him I wasn't she, and within a few minutes, this six-foot-tall, overweight woman walked in. She had false eyelashes out to her nose, and she looked like anything but a sales trainer. Then she spoke and removed all doubt. Her grammar was very poor and laced with "des," "dems," and "doses" throughout her short sentences. Had I known her earlier, I think I would have been a little insulted that Sid thought I was she! But in his defense, he had never met her.

Trudy and I asked that we be interviewed together after we told Alice we were sisters. Midway through the interview, Sid came into the office. He just sat there listening to the interview. Alice was telling us all about the Gloria Marshall operation. Gloria and her husband, Alan Bergendahl, had started the company, which now had more than 20 salons in California. They needed an infusion of money to form a new company named Body Contour, Inc. Sid had supplied the needed cash, and for his investment Sid was made a 50 percent partner and president of the new company.

Both companies operated as Gloria Marshall Figure Salons, featuring a new concept of isometric exercise without effort. The machines did the work for you. The foundation of the program was the Circlamatic that they had designed and patterned after the Stauffer toning tables, which were developed by Bernard H. Stauffer in the late 1930s. Stauffer had discovered that people could improve their posture by aligning their various body parts.

Stauffer tables were divided into four parts: one for the legs, one for the top of the legs to the waist, one for the waist to the shoulders, and a headrest. The 4 sections of the table rotated, alternating clockwise and counterclockwise. Sandbags were placed on top of the body to hold it in place: The table was intended to be a resistance machine that would promote isometric exercise. Stauffer opened a salon in Los Angeles with his sister Sally, and his first patrons discovered that not only did the tables alleviate their sore muscles and improve their muscle tone, but they soon lost inches off their thighs, stomach, hips, and arms!

The Circlamatic was a variation of the Stauffer tables. The Gloria Marshall machines used the same approach as Stauffer, but without the sandbags: They relied on the person's own body weight to hold them in place. Because my whole indoctrination into the world of exercise emphasized the philosophy of "no pain, no gain," and this new concept did not require much physical effort, I was skeptical—to say the least.

When we got to the point of compensation and opportunity, Alice threw out a figure that I thought was a joke. She said they were willing to pay us $400 a month as salon managers. Trudy looked at me and we both started laughing. Surely Alice couldn't be serious. As part owner of my own gym, I had earned $30,000 plus a year. Trudy was then working for Silhouette and earning about $20,000, which was pretty good in the 1960s. We terminated the interview and went home after a brief discussion of why we had responded to the ad and not told each other.

The next day, Sid called me at home. He said he couldn't believe how poorly Alice had handled the interview. He explained that he couldn't offer me a franchise at that time because his company was based in California, and that state required a two-year track record before he could franchise. He pleaded with me to come to work, promising me an increase in pay and the opportunity for a much higher position and eventual franchise. He had

48

taken the liberty to call his partner Alan for approval to offer me $800 a month, an amount that was unheard-of before in that company. Alan responded to his request, "Even God isn't worth $800," but I guess Sid was convincing.

> I was willing to invest the time
> in order to gain experience
> and to prepare myself for
> having my own franchise.

I was willing to invest the time in order to gain experience and to prepare myself for having my own franchise. It helped that Bobby earned a good living, and we didn't need my salary to put bread on the table. One of his strategies was to build a house doing a lot of the work himself, and then we'd live in it for a while and sell it at a good profit. Although this was a profitable procedure, it required that we move often while still remaining in the same area of the city so as not to disrupt our children's education. Because my salary was added income but wasn't required for our lifestyle, I decided to take Sid up on his offer. He also called Trudy, but she had already taken another position.

The Franchise Not Taken

At the same time, I had another example of how one decision, one turn, can lead you in a whole different direction. Three months before answering that Gloria Marshall ad, I had responded to another ad I saw in the newspaper. The ad was offering a franchise for a cosmetic salon. I was interviewed by Jerry O'Neil, who owned Janeal Cosmetique, located on St. Charles Avenue in New Orleans.

Jerry had devised a method of peeling the skin with a special formula. I was amazed when I saw the results. After she did my face it felt like a baby's skin and had a radiant glow. I was sold on the method, but I didn't know anything about the cosmetic business and I told her so. I didn't even wear makeup until I was 30 years old. I don't mean to be egotistical, but I didn't really need a lot of makeup at that time. I did wear mascara and lipstick and maybe a little blush, but I didn't use foundation or any skin-care products— none of that stuff. I told her that, but she was undaunted and said, "I can teach you that."

I went home and explained to Bobby all about it. I really liked Jerry's concept, so I went back to her and said, "I'll tell you what I'll do. I'll come to work for you . . . and you don't have to pay me a salary. Just give me 30 percent of anything I sell or do [in terms of services and products] over what you've been doing. That will give me a chance to see if I can do this and how profitable it will be, before I commit to buying a franchise."

So that's what I did: I ended up working there long enough to see whether I could do it . . . and during the first month, I increased the gross by 20 percent; by the end of the third month, I had tripled the gross sales. The new method of skin resurfacing was becoming very popular, and the outward displays of satisfaction from the clients told me that there was a future in that business. Clearly, this business *was* worth my investment.

I decided I would take the franchise, but when I approached Jerry she said, "Look, I need an assistant. I cannot travel because of my respiratory condition. How would you like to be my assistant? You could make a lot more money, and it would really help me out." Jerry was a lovely woman, but she was not well. She had developed a severe respiratory condition after she had started her business. She lived in Texas and could no longer travel because she had to carry an oxygen tank around with her.

I felt bad for her, and I appreciated her offer, but I told her, "I don't think I can do that; I just don't. I'll go home and consider it, but I don't think I could travel, with my children being at an age where they still need day-to-day supervision." (Denise was 14 years old and Michelle was only 10.) Jerry wanted me to travel all over the country: She was going to run ads in all the Southern states, and if someone expressed an interest in buying a franchise, then I would have to go there and sell it to them. If they bought it, I'd have to show them what to do to bring in customers and increase sales. I would have been on the road *all the time*, which I felt I just couldn't do. I told her I couldn't accept the position she was offering, and then she began to reconsider my purchase of the New Orleans franchise.

It was on the day of my last conversation with Jerry that I looked in the paper and read Sid's ad for Gloria Marshall, and I thought, "Gee, this sounds interesting." I don't remember the exact wording of his ad, but it gave the impression that his company had developed a new concept: passive equipment, with no need to sweat to lose weight. The way he worded the ad was provocative, so I wanted to check it out before making a decision about Jerry's franchise. I've often wondered what I'd be doing now if I had signed that franchise agreement with Jerry. I wonder whatever happened to her? Life is unpredictable!

Training to Learn a New Business

We began our Gloria Marshall training at the Arthur Murray Studio on St. Charles Avenue. Sid owned the studio, and because the salons were still under construction, he used the Arthur Murray training classroom. Sid had worked for Arthur Murray since his college days, starting out as a dance instructor and then going on to become a manager, and then a company director and owner of several franchised areas throughout the country. When he bought into the Gloria Marshall business, he still had an interest in the New Orleans studio, though he later sold it.

We were able to do our training there, because the dance students took classes at night, after work, whereas we were training during the day. Also, we didn't use the main ballroom for our training classes; there were other rooms more suitable for our purposes.

It was all I could do to bite my tongue during those first days of training. This is not ego talking, but I had *forgotten* more about sales than Alice knew.

I really tried to be a good student and pretend that Alice was an expert on the subject. She would demonstrate segments of the salon tour, but she never gave a start-to-finish demonstration. It was so confusing as to the order in which things were to be done. Alice would call on different students to give demonstrations, and it became obvious that she was not teaching them anything. Before the week was up, students were coming to me for advice. I could sense her immediate resentment toward me.

I hope in this story I haven't come across as a pompous jerk. Truly, that was not the case. I tried to genuinely appreciate her efforts, and my only goal was to be successful in the business. I have held many training classes over the years and I've found that people learn best by example. In my training classes, I show them how it should be done and then invite them to copy it. When I asked Alice if she would demonstrate how to present the program to a client, she refused by saying, "I know how to do it, *you* need to show me *you* know how, too." Because we had never seen the right way to do it, we had to improvise.

I did better than most of the students because of my previous experience working at Silhouette and in my own gym. Nevertheless, that training experience taught me a valuable lesson in leadership. A commander who isn't willing to lead his troops and set the right example isn't worth his salt in my mind. I also subscribe to the philosophy that "if the learner hasn't learned, then the teacher hasn't taught."

A commander who isn't willing to lead his troops and set the right example isn't worth his salt . . . "if the learner hasn't learned, then the teacher hasn't taught."

After training, I was appointed manager of the Westside salon. There were two program directors working with me. They were both young and eager to learn. I worked on training them every free minute we had.

As our salon sales figures began to climb, word got to Alice that I was training my two program directors, and Alice came to the salon in a huff and reprimanded me for doing her job. I realized then that she just didn't want me to be successful. Only a fool would resent help and proper training from someone who had successfully run her own business and was the person responsible for production and the success of that center!

I went to Sid and told him it was either Alice or me. I could no longer work for someone who was that narrow-minded and demotivating. He sent Alice back to California. I was appointed the area supervisor, and I began a training program that must have worked, because within months the New Orleans salons were grossing *double* what the California ones were doing. Gloria even called me to ask what my secret was. I gave her a simple answer: "Any business is simply four walls and people." If you make it easy for your employees to understand the work they're supposed to do, and if you train people well and let them know what is expected of them, then success will come. Some months later when Gloria and Alan opened the Memphis area, they called me to go there to do their training. I accepted!

Any business is simply four walls and people. . . .
If you train people well and
let them know what is expected of them,
then success will come.

Increasing Sales and Moving Up

Another lesson I learned while Alice was in charge in New Orleans was never assign to your employees a job that's impossible to accomplish. It not only limits their chances for success, but it also can damage their confidence and impair their self-image and self-worth. Alice had put a price on the program of $1,500, which was very expensive in 1970. All during her training, she talked about how in California all programs were paid in cash. And we all believed her.

Never assign to your employees
a job that's impossible to accomplish.
It not only limits their chances for success,
but it also can damage their
confidence and impair
their self-image and self-worth.

But my previous experience with the socioeconomic level of people in New Orleans told me that this price was going to be difficult for most to pay. I asked Alice if we could arrange a budget program if someone couldn't afford the lump sum all at once. She said absolutely not. So with a positive attitude I thought, "If they can do it in California, we can do it here."

Still, the first 15 or 20 people I interviewed did not buy. It would have been easy to get discouraged and quit had I not had my previous success in sales. Most of the other people working in all four salons were thinking they were not qualified for the job and were getting discouraged.

I explained to Sid that I had been in the business for so many years and had never had so many no-sales. I asked him if we could have an introductory program for those who couldn't afford the whole program. I also told him I knew some people who would finance the whole program for those clients who needed to do so. He understood the problem and agreed to do as I asked. That was a turning point in our success rate. Practically everyone enrolled after those changes.

I later found out that Alice had apparently lied about the expensive cash programs in California. I believe that for any company to be successful, its employees must be successful and feel like they're contributing something meaningful. Also, success depends on making it easy for a client to buy. The fewer obstacles you put in the way of a purchase, the easier it will be for the purchaser to buy. Alice had put unnecessary obstacles in the way, almost guaranteeing failure.

Within 18 months, we were opening new salons and expanding into other regions of the South. And I was supervising the whole Southern region. We were making history with our success! My new career was well established, and I was proud of our achievement.

But things were not so good at home. Bobby seemed to resent my work and my success. I was always careful not to bring work home, and I spent the weekends focusing on the family. I devoted the same intense focus on work during the week. I always told my employees not to call me at home unless the salon was on fire. And I told my children not to call me at work unless it was an emergency. I thought those guidelines were working well, but it didn't seem to help my marriage.

In Bobby's defense, I think he was lonely because I was working very hard and I would get home after nine o'clock every weekday. At one point, I even offered to quit my job in order to save my marriage but I soon realized that wasn't the answer.

I think accepting my marriage was failing was one of the biggest challenges I've faced in my personal life. I was trying to balance my career and take care of my kids, and I didn't know what to do about my relationship with Bobby. Do I remain in the marriage or leave?

In the summer of 1975, Sid asked if I would consider opening the Chicago market. Sid lived in Los Angeles, where the company was headquartered, so I rarely saw him after the initial opening. As I remember it, we met only twice after that—at Christmastime in 1970 when he came back to New Orleans and invited Bobby and me to dinner with him and his wife Irene, and then in 1973 when Sid asked me to go out to California for the grand openings of more salons within his company. During the five years we had worked together we did talk on the phone often, but it was always business conversations. He would call to see how things were going or to ask my opinion on something, so we had a cordial business relationship. Along the way we developed trust and respect for each other. Our conversations were usually brief because Sid always called during working hours and I was usually busy with clients.

Sid's invitation for me to open the Chicago market would mean that I, along with my family, would have to move. He explained the opportunities for advancement within the company and he made me an offer that was hard to turn down. I asked him to give me a couple of days to think it over. What Sid didn't know then was that I was thinking of getting a divorce from Bobby because things had gotten a lot worse at home. The children were old enough that I didn't think it would be too traumatic for them. I felt I needed to make a change.

Expanding the Business and Moving to Chicago

In our conversations on the phone, Sid and I had never discussed our personal lives. Our topics were always related to the business. He didn't have a clue how things were between Bobby and me or what I was thinking regarding a possible move to Chicago. As I considered his offer, I thought Chicago would be a good place to begin a new life after leaving the old one behind. I thought of the benefits of not having to deal with the loyalty of Bobby's and my friends with "our" friends becoming "his" friends and "my" friends when we separated and divorced. For other reasons, too, I accepted Sid's offer.

So in August of 1975, I packed my car with my two girls and only the things we felt we really needed and drove to Chicago. Denise was 20 years old and had already decided to attend the University of Indiana at Bloomington. Michelle was 16 years old and in high school, so I had to find a new school for her. Nick King, who was in charge of construction and the acquisition of new locations for the company, helped us. Nick was a fun guy and proved to be a really good friend. The company had leased an apartment for me and the girls in Schaumberg, Illinois, which was considered to be a central location to the 11 salons I would be opening. Once the girls were settled, I went to work.

Opening so many salons at one time proved to be tougher

than I had expected. I was grateful for having a high-energy metabolism, because it was really put to the test. The combination of interviewing prospective employees and training them while monitoring progress on the building and interior renovation of new salons was a full plate. I needed to hire five people for each of the 11 salons we were opening: a program director who handled sales, a manager, and three instructors to teach clients how to use the equipment.

> Opening so many
> salons at one time
> proved to be tougher
> than I had expected.

Most of the equipment was considered to be passive in that it did not require physical exertion to operate it. In addition to the Circlamatic, which required some resistance, there were barrel-like rollers and vibrating belts very much like those found in most gyms. In addition there were Exercycle bikes that worked most muscle groups while offering some aerobic benefit. We also had an isometric machine to help tone the muscles. Each salon had about 15 pieces of equipment. The Circlamatics were in open-front booths, giving patrons a degree of privacy for about 20 minutes. All the other equipment was in the open workout area.

My job was to interview, hire, and train all the employees necessary for the opening of the salons. In addition to training them on the equipment and its use, I had to train them in sales and bookkeeping that was all done by hand in those precomputer days. The greatest challenge in training new people in customer relations is to stress the importance of sticking to the script. In doing so, they will avoid making misleading statements. I have always believed in telling clients exactly what they can expect to get for their investment and what we expect them to do in return. That way there are no surprises and no unnecessary disappointments.

In my training classes I depended heavily on role play because it places the employee in the client's position (since they switch roles of the program director and the client), and it allows me to see whether the employee is using dialogue that is appropriate. If not, we have to go back to the drawing board with more training. Remember my philosophy: If the learner hasn't learned, then the teacher hasn't taught. When intelligent people were not performing well in class, I held myself personally responsible.

One of the most difficult things to teach people is to be concise in their dialogue. Time is important both to the client and to the employee. Many people waffle so much in their explanation of things it creates confusion and distrust, not to mention the extra time it takes to get through the presentation.

I have been asked many times, "What do you look for when hiring an employee?" Certainly experience is important, but in an industry that is relatively small we rarely get experienced people applying. When hiring, I looked for employees with people skills, and probably the number one thing I looked for was high energy combined with enthusiasm. If an applicant had experience, great, but some of our best salespeople were former teachers, nurses, and waitresses. One of the reasons for that is that in their prior careers they learned how to communicate with people. Selling is nothing more than communicating. A client communicates a need, and the employee communicates a solution. We had many excellent people working for us; in fact, many of the people employed in the Body

Contour company came to work in the Jenny Craig company and were welcomed with open arms.

> # When hiring, I looked for employees with people skills, and probably the number one thing I looked for was high energy combined with enthusiasm.

When we first started the company, we could advertise for "trim women." Now, of course, we would not be allowed to do that. Regardless of how we worded the ad, if I found someone whom I thought would be terrific in the business, even if she was slightly overweight, I hired her if she agreed to go on the program. We couldn't have people who weighed 200 pounds, but we weren't looking for Twiggy, either. It's actually a lot easier, when you're selling someone something, if you're a role model or a testimonial for your product or service. Have you ever seen a person with bad skin working at a cosmetic counter in any department store? Neither have I!

I always felt that having something in common with my customers helped me in my career, first when I was at Home Decorators and I was close to the age of the girls I was calling on, and later in the weight-management business, because I could say, "I've been there"; clients who came to lose weight knew my story and felt, "Well, she understands." I've always preferred to hire people who are healthy looking, because if you have a lot of skinny people working in any weight-loss operation, clients feel like, "What does *she* know about it? *She's* never had a weight problem in her life." We hired more mature people who had a healthy weight, rather than being skinny.

I think that's what's wrong today. The expectation of teenagers is unrealistic: Who are their role models? Fashion models are *so thin*; most people have no chance of ever achieving that because of their genetics or their lifestyles.

We finally managed to staff the salons with reasonably trained people, and we celebrated our grand openings.

Expanding the Midwest Operation

The Chicago area was not an immediate success. We were not doing what we had expected to do in the way of gross sales, and I didn't know why, because we were getting a lot of leads. After spending much time going from one location to the other, training more on a one-to-one basis, I was baffled as to why we were not doing better. I scanned the records, and bingo, it hit me.

In our contract, we had a clause that said the cost of a program must be paid within 90 days. To new employees, who will usually take the avenue of least resistance, the wording on the contract meant they could let clients drag out the payments for 90 days, rather than pay the full amount up front, so they did. Virtually every enrollment fee was spread over 90 days, so we had to go back to square one in training. Having clients pay the full amount is both good for the company and good for the client. Just as with school tuition, when someone makes a full financial commitment, he or she is more likely to complete the program in order to get the full benefit of their investment.

With that adjustment, the salons soon began to turn in super figures (no pun intended). The valuable lesson I learned from that experience is that because people will always take the avenue of least resistance, make sure *you* can live with the terms of the contract you offer. When given too much flexibility, most people will take the easy way every time.

We continued to open new salons, and before long we had 30 salons in the greater Chicago area. Chicago became the highest-grossing area in the company; it became the standard for excellence. We were advertising on the morning show, doing *live* commercials because the show's hosts became avid supporters after seeing so many testimonials to the efficacy of our program. Even the female mayor, Jane Byrne, was using the Body Contour program. Chicago continued to lead the nation in sales throughout the 1970s.

In November 1975, the company held its first national convention. Sid chose Chicago as the location, thinking that would help to motivate the new people. After arriving in Chicago, he invited me out to dinner. When we met at the restaurant, Sid asked me, "Where's your husband? Isn't he coming?" I told him my husband had not moved with me and that we were going through a divorce. He looked at me and started to laugh. He then told me that he and Irene had separated and he, too, had filed for divorce.

At some point during that convention, I began to see Sid as a man and not just as a boss. It was the first time we had conversations dealing with personal matters. He stayed in Chicago for a week, and we had a lot of fun together. By the time he left to return to California, we had a whole different kind of relationship. Soon after, he invited me out to California for the weekend. I accepted and that was the beginning of our cross-country courtship.

For three years, I continued to work very hard securing the Chicago area's top position within the company. But I also made time for other activities that were important to me. For example, while I was in Chicago, I took several courses at the University of Chicago. I didn't need a degree, because I already had the top job within the company that I could have in Chicago: I was supervising Chicago, and later, Cleveland—almost 50 centers, which was like running a company within a company. I took a course in nutrition, because I was interested in knowing more about it, but I didn't feel there was any need for me to become a nutritionist; moreover, the rewards for that were certainly nothing like what I was earning. People usually change career directions either for money or for circumstances—for example, if they have to move to a new region and change careers—but I didn't have either of those situations, so there was no reason for me to consider any other direction in my career.

I also took anthropology courses simply because I was fascinated by the topic; I like learning new things and discovering new things. I took the courses only for audit, because I didn't have time to study and be tested; I simply wanted the information from those courses.

I took French simply because I was interested in it. I had spoken French before I spoke English as a child because my parents spoke it at home: My mother's family was from around the Pyrenees, and my father's people also were from France, so they spoke what I called "Gumbo French": It was French mixed in with Cajun. When I went to school as a girl, I didn't want any part of speaking a foreign language. But then later, after Denise studied French, I became interested again.

At some point along the way, my sister Trudy came to work for the company. She first started working in the New Orleans area. After a while, Sid asked her to open the salons in the Ohio Valley, beginning in Cincinnati. She accepted his offer and moved to Ohio. Sid asked me to go there to help her with the grand openings.

Trudy had rented a house for out-of-town employees. I stayed there with her and three others who were sent from California. I can't remember ever laughing so much as we all did during our stay there. One of the women (Marie) was a tall, willowy, and very thin blonde with a beautiful California tan. We were all working long hours at a fast pace, but Marie had never worked hard in her life.

Our first clue was when she came to work with a diamond ring that would choke a horse, high heels, and designer clothes. Because she was not accustomed to hard work, she developed these huge blisters on her feet, the result of working in high heels. Every night she would walk in the door, legs bowed, and show us how the blisters were getting bigger. I suggested that she ditch the high heels and wear more sensible shoes and while she was at it put her diamond ring in a safety deposit box, but I don't think she took my advice on either suggestion.

My sister Trudy had always been very naive. When Marie would tell us about life in Hollywood, Trudy would look a little confused or say something to indicate she didn't understand what Marie was talking about. Marie would look at me and ask, "Is your sister for real or is this an act?" She decided to find out for herself. She asked Trudy, "Do you know what uppers and downers are?" Trudy answered, "Of course, they're dentures. Everybody knows that." Well, we all fell off our chairs laughing after realizing that she was dead serious. There were many evenings that went like that. After that trip, Marie and her experiences would cause Trudy and me to double over in laughter in remembering her vivid descriptions. I stayed in Cincinnati for about three weeks, and then returned to Chicago.

Next, I opened the Cleveland area with Gloria Marshall salons. My division was growing rapidly. My job, once again, was to recruit and train people for seven grand openings in Cleveland, only this time it had to be done while I was also supervising the Chicago area. I couldn't have done it had I not developed dedicated, well-trained people whom I could depend on to do a great job in Chicago.

It has always puzzled me why some people put so little emphasis on trying to duplicate themselves. It's so obvious to me that in order to advance to a higher position, you must have a qualified replacement. To me, the most significant achievement for any supervisor is the development of other good people like her- or himself. It's sad that some people feel threatened by others who are equally talented. I have always found that talented people working for you make *you* look better because they contribute so much to the overall success of the project.

> Some people put so little emphasis
> on trying to duplicate themselves. . . .
> To advance to a higher position,
> you must have a qualified replacement.

In 1978, I was promoted as the chief operations officer (COO) for Body Contour Inc., only without the official title. That meant I would have to move to California, where the company's headquarters were based. I looked forward to doing so after three very cold winters in Chicago. Even though my office on Michigan Avenue was only three blocks from my apartment, there were mornings I had to take a taxi because the wind chill factor was minus 45 degrees, and the wind was so strong, it was difficult to walk without being blown away. The thought of sunny, warm weather was certainly a welcome idea. Not the least cause of my excitement was the fact that I would be closer to Sid. By that time, we were very much in love.

That same year, the company decided to hold our national convention in Cincinnati, because the Ohio Valley was the newest region. Up to that point, Sid and I had kept our personal relationship private. Although some people may have suspected, we had never told anyone that our relationship was anything more than a business relationship between good friends.

But as we were driving back to our hotel on the last evening of the convention (Sid, Trudy, and I, and Jim McCormick, who ran the marketing division of the company), Sid turned to Trudy and said, "Trudy, I am in love with your little sister." Those were the first words of admission that either of us had spoken publicly. I'll never forget the look on Trudy's face. She was completely surprised. I was also surprised that he chose to tell her in that way, but he wanted her to know before rumors started flying throughout the company.

From then on, it was no secret that Sid and I were in love. We wanted people to know it was not just a frivolous flirtation between boss and employee. In a company with more than 400 women (many of whom were single) and no men other than Sid and Alan, who was married to Gloria, you can imagine the kind of rumors that could develop. And we were careful not to flaunt our relationship during working hours or at company gatherings.

Another funny thing happened during that visit to Cincinnati. While Sid and Trudy were having a breakfast meeting one morning, the subject of franchising came up. Sid was ranting on about how his experience with Elsie had discouraged him from ever franchising his business again. He called her "a bitch from hell." Trudy couldn't let that pass, and she told him that Elsie was our sister. I wish I could have been a fly on the wall to witness that moment. Trudy told me he just put his fork down, pushed his food away, and never ate another bite. He remained speechless. We all still laugh about how that inevitable event happened.

I moved out to California in 1978, and later that year, Sid's divorce became final. It had taken three years. He asked me to marry him, and we made plans to be married by a rabbi with a reception following at the Pacifica Hotel. When Sid told his mother of the upcoming wedding, she advised us to go to Las Vegas instead because she thought a big wedding would be hard for his three children: Jason was only 7 years old, Steven was 11, and Susan was 12. We took her advice and we were married on February 18, 1979, in Las Vegas, Nevada. And we had a very small wedding; we invited just a few of our friends to attend. Caesars Palace provided a royal feast and everything was complimentary (that's when you know you're a pigeon). Caesars was "the" hotel in those days.

Two weeks later, while we were lounging around in our apartment, the telephone rang and Sid answered. The voice on the other end asked, "Mr. Craig?" Sid learned he was talking to the rabbi who was to have married us. It seems we had failed to call him to cancel our original plans, so the rabbi was at the hotel waiting for us so he could perform the ceremony. Even though Sid made a sizable donation to his synagogue, it was still embarrassing, to say the least, but over the years we've learned to laugh about it. As you can probably tell, our life together has always been filled with humor.

In 1978, when I made the permanent move to the West Coast, we stayed at the hotel Sid had been living in. We were there for only a short time because the apartment had very little closet space for my clothes.

Sid is a very lovable character. He has the charisma of a Jack Kennedy, the intelligence of an Alan Greenspan, the creative mind of a Steven Spielberg, and the humor of a Jackie Mason, along with the good looks of a Clark Gable. His mind is constantly working at top speed. Early on in our marriage, Sid would wake up during the night with an idea. He sleeps very little as he is an insomniac. While he would describe the idea, I would listen attentively; if it sounded like a good project, I would immediately start thinking of how to develop or implement it. After researching and planning for a few days I'd go to Sid and say, "Here's how I see it working." He'd look at me with a puzzled look and say, "Oh, *that* idea. Well, I have a *better* idea," and he would proceed to introduce something that had nothing to do with his previous idea.

I have always been a *doer* so when I'm given a project, I immediately get to work on it. Sid, on the other hand, gets as much fulfillment just *thinking* it through as he would *seeing* it through to fruition.

It took me a while to adjust to the way his mind creates and discards ideas like yesterday's news. I've learned to listen and then let the dust settle before reacting. That technique has saved me a lot of time and effort.

Sid tells the story about his early days in Arthur Murray when every other day he would go to his boss with a new idea. He did this so much that one day when he went to his boss with one of his ideas, his boss stopped him midsentence and said, "I have a better idea . . . *gross, gross, and more gross.*"

Our life together has been exciting, fun, and interesting. We share many of the same interests. We enjoy people and manage to surround ourselves with many whose friendship we value. We have a keen interest in business and marketing. We enjoy sports, and only a family emergency would keep us from Monday night football. We play tennis and we recently added golf to our activities. We cherish the time we spend with our family, and we try to all get together as often as possible. With five children and their spouses and 12 grandchildren, we represent a crowd wherever we are.

My dad used to say, "In life there are *givers* and *takers*; always be a *giver*." I believe Sid and I are both *givers*. Sid would much rather do something for someone else than have them do something for him. I feel the same way. Sometimes it can be difficult to do things for Sid because it seems to make him uncomfortable to accept acts of love that include any kind of help or assistance.

Sid is also fiercely loyal. He has maintained close relationships with many of his college buddies. He has a couple of friends that he has known since grammar school and he still keeps in touch with them. Jerry Tarkanian (the famous basketball coach) was Sid's roommate in college. Jerry has often said, "One thing I really admire about Sid is that in spite of his great success, he has never forgotten his friends."

Sid and I . . . worked together in the same office,
but we never got in each other's way.
We tried to always have clearly
defined areas of responsibility.

Sid and I have had a happy marriage since day one. It isn't often that a couple can spend 24 hours a day together without occasional friction. We worked together in the same office, but we never got in each other's way. We tried to always have clearly defined areas of responsibility. Perhaps, though, the main reason it has worked for us is that each of us has a great amount of respect for the other's talents and credibility. I've always believed that with respect comes love, so I guess that's what started our lifelong love affair.

4

Negotiating a Buyout

"I'd rather be in jail than be here."

In early 1981, Sid and I recognized that our industry was changing. People were beginning to pay attention to what they ate. Up
to that point, no one thought that what you ate would affect the
way you looked or how you felt. They really thought that you could
eat anything you want. Who ever heard of vegetarians before the
1970s, except maybe the flower children who ushered this in, in the
1960s? But by 1981, there was so much research and information
about how diet affects our weight and our bodies that people were
finally beginning to pay attention to the kinds of foods they ate.

I had learned most of what was being talked about long before
then through my experience in the industry and the research I had
done with what little information was available. But thankfully that
information was becoming mainstream. So Sid and I went to Gloria
Marshall and told her we thought we ought to include a lot more
about nutrition in the program. At that time, the only thing we
were offering was a grapefruit diet, which of course is a fad diet—
and those things don't work. They might take pounds off for a little
while, but not for long. We wanted to incorporate a more healthful
eating regimen.

Sid went to Alan Bergendahl and Gloria and emphasized the importance of incorporating a sensible diet plan to work along with the machines. They rejected our suggestion. They felt that things were going well, and their response was, "If something ain't broke, don't fix it." And that was the end of the conversation; there was no further discussion. But I knew if we didn't change our direction soon, another company would do it and render our program obsolete.

> I knew if we didn't change our direction soon,
> another company would do it
> and render our program obsolete.

We didn't know for a fact that there was any specific competitor, but the writing was on the wall: We knew that someone was going to introduce a program of diet and nutrition. Weight Watchers, in those days, was not very well known. It was out there, but it wasn't the company it is today, or anywhere close. It was like a neighborhood gathering, which is how the company started. They would hold meetings, usually once a week, in garages and in homes. In those days, they didn't do a lot of advertising; they ran little notices in the paper, saying there would be a Weight Watchers meeting on Tuesday at such-and-such a location.

I also knew that machines alone or even physical exercise alone were not enough. A healthy diet was essential to weight loss and a healthy body.

Sid and I decided we had different motivations from Gloria and Alan, and we tried to do everything we could to go along with their way, but finally we went back to them and offered some options: (1) we would buy them out, (2) they could buy us out, or (3) we would split the salons in half. Their reply was, "No, we like the arrangement just the way it is." So we were left with only one alternative: to sell the company to an outside party. Sid had talked to our attorney and was presented the option of an involuntary dissolution if the Bergendahls refused to go along.

In 1981, we contacted Merrill Lynch to find a buyer for our business, and we soon had some very big companies looking at us: H&R Block, Gillette, and others came to check out our operation and meet with us. But we didn't make any headway, because once these companies began to understand our business, they didn't think it would fit in with their own organizations.

Then Sid remembered reading an article in the paper about Harold Katz, who was the chairman of NutriSystem. Its stock was trading in the area of half a billion dollars on the New York Stock Exchange. We didn't know a lot about the company, but we knew the type of program it offered: NutriSystem had a food program called "Food 2000" or "21st Century Food" (the impression was that it was space-age types of food), and there was no exercise involved. NutriSystem presented its program as a medical type of program. So in the fall of 1981, Sid decided to forget about the broker, and he cold-called Harold Katz. Sid, from our kitchen phone, reached Harold at home, on *his* kitchen phone. Sid explained the whole situation—where we were with our business and how the partnership with Alan and Gloria wasn't working out anymore.

Harold invited us out to his corporate offices in Philadelphia to meet and talk about our fit with their company. Sid and I went about a week later—this was in November 1981—and we stayed for the weekend. We had a meeting in Harold's office, with about 10 people from NutriSystem: his advertising people, his attorney, a couple of franchisees. We talked about the Gloria Marshall program and how it worked. They asked a lot of questions, and the more we talked, the more excited Harold was getting. We also went out to dinner with Harold and he seemed to be really interested.

After that first meeting, Sid said there was no doubt in his mind that this was going to be a deal, because it was so obvious that Harold wanted our company. It was different from when we met with Gillette or H&R Block, so Sid dealt directly with the principals at NutriSystem, without the Merrill Lynch broker.

Within a month after we were back in California, Harold called and said he wanted to come out to visit us at our corporate offices in Downey for a bit of due diligence and to take a closer look at our operation. He came with his attorney and a financial person, and they looked all around the home office and visited a few of the salons.

Prior to Harold's arrival Sid told Gloria and Alan that he had talked to Harold and that he seemed to be interested. The Bergendahls didn't object to *selling* the company; they just didn't want to change it, and they didn't want us to have it. But if someone from outside came and offered them money, they weren't opposed to that. So they also met with Harold.

During this meeting Alan kept leaving the room without explanation; at one point, he even fell asleep. We could see Harold was getting annoyed. What he didn't know at the time was that Alan was a severe diabetic, and it was not uncommon for him to nod off in the middle of a conversation. Still, Harold said if he had met Alan and Gloria first he never would have been interested in acquiring our company, and we never would have had a second meeting. He said he didn't blame us for wanting out of that situation. It was a perfect example of how you never get a second chance to make a first impression.

So we all agreed to sell the company to NutriSystem. The paperwork to complete the deal was enormous, because Gloria and Alan had 17 corporations that they needed to unwind from the deal, and they wanted to keep their businesses that were in Australia, so they needed to spin out the salons that were located there. Still, the deal was wrapped up pretty quickly; only about six months passed from the time of Sid's first phone call to Harold. It all happened so quickly because Harold was so intent on getting the company; he felt that he could really do something with it. He had his attorneys fly in from Philadelphia to push through the deal, because he really wanted to buy our company. He was anxious. After a lot of haggling and mounds of paperwork, we had a deal. I was glad to be out from under our partnership with the Bergendahls because I really felt that the Body Contour program was becoming too stagnant, and the Bergendahls were becoming too difficult for us to deal with. I believe you either move forward or you move backward; you can't stand still in the business world. You've got to do *something*, and we weren't moving forward.

> I believe you either move forward
> or you move backward;
> you can't stand still in the business world.
> You've got to do *something*.

Working for Someone Else—Again

Part of the agreement with Harold was that Sid and I would move to Philadelphia during the transition. That meant signing a management contract with $500,000 held in escrow guaranteeing our performance. Excluded from the sale were the Australian salons that the Bergendahls owned. They continued to operate the Gloria Marshall salons there.

I didn't mind moving from California to Philadelphia, because it wasn't going to be for a long time, only for a year. Plus, I like challenges, and I like traveling. Sid didn't expect it was going to be as bad as it turned out to be for him, because Harold had made a lot of promises to him: "Nothing's going to change; you're going to run the company just like you have been; you'll be in separate buildings from our offices; you'll be handling everything: the advertising and so on." I would continue doing the field training. The only difference was supposed to be in the relocation.

I thought it would be different from when I sold Healthletic to Silhouette, because we had a stronger motivation to sell our business this time. When Adele and I sold our gym to our former employers, I wasn't unhappy with what I was *doing*: I was going from running a successful business that I enjoyed to working for people I didn't particularly want to work for. But in this case, I felt I had no reason to worry: I liked Harold, and I thought, if we're still going to be running this business just as we've been doing, then why not sell? Plus, we would have money in our pocket, to boot! So I really didn't have a negative attitude about the move; in fact, I was kind of excited. I thought it would be fun to go to Philadelphia and see the difference we could make without working with the Bergendahls. It seemed to me like starting a new company.

But when we got to Philadelphia, things were immediately different from what we expected. To say that Philadelphia was challenging is a gross understatement. Because our offices were located in a different building in another part of town than were the NutriSystem corporate offices, we rarely even saw Harold during working hours. We did have dinner with him on several occasions and we attended other social functions. Harold owned the Philadelphia 76ers basketball team, and we attended a couple of games with him. Although I liked Harold socially, he had some ideas in business that directly conflicted with my basic values of how to treat people, especially women employees.

For instance, soon after the papers were signed, he came to the Body Contour, Inc., convention in April 1982 to announce the sale of the company and to introduce his key executives. Every year, we held a convention, sort of a rah-rah meeting for Body Contour, Inc., franchisees and employees from all over the country. We had motivational speakers, we might introduce a new piece of equipment, and we would also give out awards and other recognition of a job well done over the past year.

We had scheduled the convention for that year, 1982, in Las Vegas, at Caesars Palace. However, in the interim, we had sold the company. Once the company was sold, Harold said he wanted to announce that he had acquired us, and he wanted to do it at our convention. We wanted to make the announcement ourselves, but Harold insisted that he would do it. He was the big honcho and he took over.

At the start of the convention, we usually convened in a large room, with long tables, in a seminar format, to kick things off. Harold got up on the stage and started to tell a lot of off-color jokes, which didn't go over very well with all of the women—and they were *all* women in the audience, or at least 99 percent of the 300 people attending were women. Then he introduced each member of his team, but there wasn't one woman among them, just men in suits. Picture a room filled with women, as one of them shouted, "Don't you have any *women* in your organization?" Harold then proceeded to introduce his secretary. I considered that to be an offensive gesture, and I'm sure many others in the room did also.

To compound his insensitivity to women, he proceeded to tell locker-room jokes that further alienated his all-female audience. He also continually referred to the employees as "girls." When he was finished talking, he sat down at a table where Sid and I were sitting. One of the employees came over and knelt down beside him and said "Mr. Katz, I would appreciate it if you would not refer to us women as 'girls.' " He turned to her and said, "If that's the only thing you got out of this convention, get your things and leave now." I was stunned and ready to challenge him, when Sid grabbed my knee and whispered, "Not here." I realized he was right that it was not the appropriate time or place to confront those issues, so I remained silent. But our interaction with Harold was very strained for the rest of the evening and throughout the rest of the convention.

When Harold made the announcement that he had bought our company, he asked that we all consider him as a "stepfather" figure. He knew we had run the company like a family business. He said that nothing would change in the working conditions. I'm sure his remarks were met with some skepticism. Throughout the first day of the convention, I think people couldn't believe we had sold the company, because they obviously didn't know about our relationship with the Bergendahls and our differences in philosophy. Thankfully, by the end of the convention, most employees believed—as we did—that the NutriSystem company could take us to higher levels and we could achieve greater things than we ever had done before. As employees' enthusiasm grew and their excitement mounted, the last evening was noisy and exuberant, causing one of the NutriSystem executives to comment, "How could you sell this company? I've never seen such enthusiasm!"

However, now that Sid and I had witnessed Harold's attitude toward women, we were having second thoughts about how it would be to work for him. Also, it was difficult for us to see tears from some of the employees as they realized that one day in the future we would no longer be there. We had always nurtured our relationships with many of the key people in our organization. So although we were happy to be free of our previous partnership, that convention was not a shining hour for us.

One reason for my concern about working for Harold was that he had created a "hit list" of all the women in the company who earned more than $50,000 a year, saying, "No broad in the world is worth $50,000." So without ever knowing what their contribution was to the company's success, he had earmarked them for termination. Two of the employees on the list were my sister Trudy and my daughter Denise.

Shortly after the conference, Sid and I left for Philadelphia. We moved into an apartment that NutriSystem had rented for us in Jenkintown, a suburb of Philadelphia, near the company headquarters. It wasn't like the home we left, of course, but we didn't mind what they had chosen for us, because we knew we were going to be there only a year; plus, we knew that we were going to be at work so much of the time that we would essentially just be sleeping there. We didn't have any friends in Philadelphia, so we weren't planning to do any entertaining.

At the same time, we allowed some of Harold's executives who were going to be operating from the Downey, California, corporate office to stay in our home there and use my car. In retrospect, that was a mistake. They trashed my car, and when we finally returned home things were missing. Not the least of those things were boxes of Christmas ornaments that I had collected over 20 plus years. I decided to just write it off as a bad decision.

Sid hated Philadelphia from the first day. We were hardly there when Harold started sending his people in. For example, NutriSystem had a certain *formula* for budgeting its advertising, and we had never believed in using formulas for advertising. Instead of looking at each market and what it was doing, they figured a certain percentage of money should be devoted to advertising, across the board—or really, across the country. But different markets require different types of advertising. And sometimes you need to have deficit spending in order to attract enough customers and maintain brand image. But NutriSystem used a formula without even looking at the market—for example, they said, "We're going to take 10 percent of the revenue a market is generating and spend that on advertising." Sid and I felt that approach followed the law of diminishing returns, because if you take 10 percent and the membership goes down, and you take 10 percent of that, then it'll go down more, because you're taking 10 percent of less money each time.

We felt that you can't advertise that way; instead, you have to look at each market, and see what you need to spend in that market to get the number of leads needed to be successful. But when Sid made those suggestions, Harold's executives totally disregarded what he said. Naturally, Sid felt rejected. He felt they placed no value on what he was saying, so he really was feeling terribly inadequate and unhappy. Every morning, he'd sit on the side of the bed, put his feet on the floor, and say, "I'd rather be in jail than be here." He was just miserable.

> You have to look at each market,
> and see what you need to spend in that market
> to get the number of leads needed
> to be successful.

Not long after our move to Philadelphia, when Sid called Harold about something to do with the business, Harold listened and then said, "My team [the 76ers] won the NBA title, and you didn't even congratulate me." Sid replied, "Gee, Harold, I was planning on doing that after we discussed this problem," but that didn't seem to appease Harold. From then on, things changed for the worse. Harold had his COO and his vice president in marketing calling all the shots. Sid and I still attended every meeting, and I could see they were discounting most of Sid's recommendations. Sid was miserable, and it showed. He was used to running a company, and he knew what worked and what didn't work in advertising. Sid's genius has always been in marketing. I attended to all the field operations, but I had always relied totally on his expertise in marketing. Harold's vice presidents had different ideas. Pretty soon,

Harold was calling me for input and at times he was very complimentary to me. I was working very hard, and things were going
well within the new company.

One day Harold called me to make a training film for
NutriSystem. I thought it strange that he didn't have a trainer
worthy enough to do it. But, in any event, I agreed to do it and
proceeded to make the film. That added fuel to Sid's feelings of
alienation. I tried my best to encourage him to keep a positive attitude about the move and the working arrangement, but in the
end I could tell the situation was making him sick. In fact, one
day about six weeks after we'd arrived in Philadelphia, Sid had a
little spell, and I took him to the emergency room. His blood
pressure had risen so high I thought he might have a stroke.
Soon after this, Sid went to talk to Harold to see if he would release us from our contract, and Harold got really incensed. Sid
came back to me and said he didn't think Harold would release
us, so he talked to Marvin, our attorney.

In the meantime, *I* decided I would go to Harold and ask him
to release us from our contract. We were willing to forfeit the escrow dollars guaranteeing our completion of the work contract. I
told him I was worried about Sid's health and I thought he was going to have a stroke. I told Harold that Sid was unhappy, and I
think Harold was unhappy with Sid because Sid didn't seem interested in the business—but Sid wasn't interested because he didn't
have any control!

Harold misread my plea and thought I was pushing for a raise in
salary. But that wasn't what I was there for, because he couldn't have
paid me enough to stay on. Harold thought I wanted more money,
because when we sold the company I had been earning more than
$150,000 a year, and Harold had told me he couldn't pay me as
much as I had been earning because my salary couldn't exceed what
his brother, a key employee, was earning at the time. I believe what
he was really saying was he couldn't pay a woman more than his

top male employees. I didn't negotiate then because Sid and I had already achieved our main objective, that of selling the company.

I believe what he was really saying was he couldn't pay a woman more than his top male employees.

Harold's response to my request that he release us from our contract was, "Look, how much do you want?" He then offered me more than his brother was earning, which was a stroke for my ego but not what I was looking for. I explained again that Sid was making himself sick and I was worried about him. Harold had been told that I had taken Sid to the emergency room with an anxiety attack. He said he'd talk to Sid about it, and he came to our office and had a meeting with Sid.

Whatever they talked about didn't seem to change Sid's feelings of rejection. Every morning he continued to repeat the same mantra, "I'd rather be in jail than be here." It was putting quite a strain on our marriage. I was waking up feeling optimistic about the day's events, and he was dragging me down. That's the only time in our 25-year marriage that I felt challenged to keep it going. Together, we went to talk to Harold again, and he said he would talk to his attorney. Finally, about four months after we had arrived in Philadelphia, Harold finally agreed to release us from our contract for a portion of the money held in escrow. Even though he wasn't happy with Sid, he still thought I was doing a terrific job. But he agreed to let us go.

It was plain to see Harold was not happy about our leaving, though I wrote out a whole schedule of all the promotions we had, internally and externally; how many leads we had; how many enrollments we had; the cash that was taken in—a whole spreadsheet so that Harold could easily see everything to compare with whatever he was planning to do in the future. I gave him as much information as I could possibly provide. We left our business affairs in great shape.

Many of Body Contour, Inc.'s key executives were leaving the company because their salaries had been slashed. NutriSystem was not doing well because the Gloria Marshall salons were not contributing to their bottom line. I have always believed that any business is simply four walls and people. No matter how great your product or service is, without good people delivering it, you have nothing. As the Gloria Marshall salons became less and less profitable and were creating a drag on the company, Harold closed many of the locations.

> ## Any business is simply four walls and people. No matter how great your product or service is, without good people delivering it, you have nothing.

Furthermore, because of their formula for advertising and the law of diminishing returns, the salons that were still open did less and less as they continued to operate in the red. Finally, the company abandoned all remaining salons by just walking away, leaving equipment and all fixtures in the salons. Some of the employees and a few landlords took over some locations and continued to operate them. I believe some of them still exist and operate, as of this writing.

Then NutriSystem's stock began to plummet, which represented an opportunity for a takeover. One of NutriSystem's top executives, Don McCullough, put a group of investors together and bought out the largest stockholder, Harold Katz. They were so successful in turning the company around that *Forbes* magazine did an article profiling McCullough and crediting him with one of the biggest turnarounds in history. I don't mean to trivialize his accomplishments, but I think timing was critical to his success, as diet and exercise were becoming more mainstream as necessary components to a healthy lifestyle. McCullough just rode along with the current.

Ready for a New Business Challenge

After the release papers were signed, we returned to California in the summer of 1982. We quickly found out that retirement isn't for everyone. But we had signed a two-year noncompete clause for North America along with the specific exclusion of Australia written in the contract, because Gloria and Alan were keeping their Australian salons out of the sale of the company.

After about two weeks, we decided we couldn't live the life of retirement and began to think about creating a whole new company: a company that would incorporate all the benefits that we knew were necessary for successful weight management. The obvious place to launch it was Australia, because doing so would not in any way violate our noncompete agreement. Even though there were Gloria Marshall salons in Australia, we wanted to develop a completely different program: We wanted to introduce nutritional guidance, behavior modification, and foods.

When somebody makes a decision to go on a diet, whether because of reading a book or on doctor's advice, they become almost totally preoccupied with food. We decided that if we provided the food, it would let the clients focus on their own bodies. Even though there was no exercise equipment in the centers we opened in Australia, we certainly recommended that our clients do exercise on their own. Still, anyone who was selling weight loss—whether it was surgery, diet pills, or anything else—was competition for us.

Sid was actually thrilled to now be competing with Alan and Gloria. While we had been involved with Body Contour, Inc., someone had come to Sid with the idea of opening salons in Australia. Sid researched it, and then he talked to Alan and Gloria about it. They ignored the idea and didn't encourage Sid to pursue it. After a few months, though, we learned they had gone to the man and dealt directly with him, cutting Sid out of the deal and doing it through another company they owned that was not part of Body Contour, Inc. What a pretty devious thing to do to a partner who had offered them participation with him! So you can see why there would be a feeling of justice as we opened our centers in competition with them in Australia. After all, turnabout is fair play!

5

The Beginning of
Jenny Craig, Inc.

"A company that would incorporate all the necessary benefits of successful weight management."

O nce we decided that the only place for us to start a new company in the same industry was Australia, we went to the Australian Consulate in Los Angeles for information. The consul told us his brother was an attorney in Melbourne, and he said his brother could open a lot of doors for us there. The consul wrote a letter about us to his brother, saying we were a very nice couple, conscientious, honest, and successful, and that we would be adding a great program to Australia. Melbourne thus was a natural place for us to start out in.

I guess I'm something of a vagabond, having relocated from New Orleans to Miami, Chicago, California, Philadelphia, and back again to California. I love to travel, and I like challenges and exciting opportunities. Ruth Meier, the nutritionist we hired in Australia, asked me once how I could move to Australia to start a new business at the age of 50. But I didn't consider 50 to be old, and I didn't think that being 50 was any more of a disadvantage than being 30!

I didn't consider 50 to be old,
and I didn't think that being 50 was
any more of a disadvantage than being
30! . . . the factors that make a business
successful have *nothing* to do with age!

After all, the factors that make a business successful have *nothing* to do with age! Sid and I knew there was a market in Australia, we knew the industry well enough, we knew the things that were important to do, and we had a few dollars that we could invest in order to achieve it. So we decided to go for it; it was as simple as that.

And I still feel that way, and I'm 71 years old at the time of this writing. Just last week, Sid and I got some information on a potential business opportunity that Sid felt was a lock to be successful, but it required someone as experienced as we are to go to Australia to get it started and up and running. And even though we don't need the money, when Sid told me this, I said, "I'll go!" I'm in great shape, I feel good, so why not? I would do it. But we have a pretty nice life here in California, so we're going to stay put, at least for the near future. (That decision worked well since the business deal that had been presented to Sid turned out to have been presented to others who immediately jumped at the opportunity.)

There is no substitute for experience when one is considering a business venture because there are pitfalls that are not so obvious to the inexperienced eye. My advice to anyone contemplating a leap into an industry they are unfamiliar with is to learn at the other person's expense. Work for a company in that industry *first*, learn the business, see what you can improve, and if your talents will add significantly to the outcome. Consider the risks before you take the plunge into a world totally unknown to you. If you find that it's not what you expected or that the reward isn't worth the risks, *don't do it!* In spending the time to learn before investing your hard-earned money, you are approaching the venture prudently.

Sometimes the secrets of success of another business are very subtle. For example, at one time, Sid had opened up a couple of hot dog stores called Dog on a Stick. Sid got into this business because he found out about someone who had 100 of these stores and was extremely successful. One of the owner's employees came to Sid and said he could duplicate exactly what the other guy had done, so he convinced Sid to go into the business. But Sid failed at it.

Later on, Sid met the guy who was so successful, and he told him that he'd failed, to which the guy said, "A lot of people tried to replicate my business, and a lot of them failed." The guy explained why: He served fresh lemonade with the hot dogs, which nobody else had ever done. Second, he didn't let his hot dogs sit around: He made them fresh for each customer, and he never served leftovers the way other hot dog businesses would.

As with many businesses, people try to cut corners here and there, to try to increase their profits. But in doing so, they destroy their loyal customer base. This guy threw out what hadn't sold at the end of the day. Because Sid didn't know this factor was important, he didn't make it a mandatory procedure.

Researching the Australian Market

We began to research food products we could develop in Australia. This was a very tedious process, because we had to take foods in the United States that were similar to what we wanted in Australia, then send samples to Australia, where they went through an inspection and incubation period of a week or two. Our attorney in Melbourne had introduced us to an Australian research company that had recommended various Australian food companies, and after the incubation period, those companies would take a shot at duplicating our foods and then send them back to us so we could taste their versions.

After much tasting and alteration, we decided on a few canned products: chili con carne, chicken soup, beef stew, and other kinds of soups; tuna salad; and chicken salad. We also had boxes of dried foods, including cereals and pancakes. We now have more than 70 varieties of foods, but we had only about 15 then, because the tasting and testing process was so arduous. Within a few months, we realized the process was taking too long. So we decided one of us should go to Australia. This was about two months after we had returned to California, in the fall of 1982.

Sid couldn't go, because shortly after we sold Body Contour, Inc., and returned to California, Sid had begun a vitamin company. It hadn't been launched yet, so he couldn't leave before doing so. Sid was still in the testing phase of the company idea: He had developed approximately seven different vitamin regimes—for example, a vegetarian plan, a weight-loss program plan, a regimen for nursing mothers, and one for pregnant women—to include whatever vitamins each person was likely to be deficient in.

A customer would complete a questionnaire describing his or her lifestyle and special nutritional needs, and a vitamin program would be designed specifically for them. The program was intended to be a drive-through process, with kiosks to be located on the grounds of regional malls.

Before he built the kiosks, Sid needed to test the service in a more cost-effective way, so he advertised in the newspapers to find out if he would get the kind of response he wanted and needed. He knew if he could sell his vitamin program through the mail, it would be successful. He ran the ads in four sections of *TV Guide*. In order to do that, though, the law required that he have 10,000 boxes of vitamins, ready to fulfill any orders that came in. Unfortunately, Sid got only 10 calls.

After realizing we needed somebody to go to Australia, and knowing Sid couldn't leave and that I couldn't do everything single-handed, we decided to take on a partner who had been Sid's friend for many years and had experience in our industry.

He and I set out for Australia, leaving Sid to complete his new vitamin venture. Our partner's responsibility was to seek out locations and organize furniture purchases for the centers as well as secure purchase agreements from various food companies. My responsibilities were to do all the things I was experienced at: develop the program, develop the classes, as well as recruit and train the people who would work in the centers.

That was one of the most stressful times of my life. Within just a few weeks, it became apparent that our partnership would not work out. I told Sid that he'd better get to Australia if he hoped to salvage our investment. By that time, Sid had realized that his vitamin company idea was a little ahead of its time because it was not showing promise to be the profitable, successful venture he had envisioned. A few years later it would have been a winner, because those types of personalized vitamins programs have been hugely successful in recent years. In any event, he wrapped up his involvement and was on a plane to Australia as quickly as possible.

Immediately upon arriving at the airport in Australia, Sid could tell there was a great need for a comprehensive weight-loss program. There was no program that addressed the benefits of a healthy diet along with an active lifestyle and behavior modification. Second, there were a lot of overweight people. We were a little surprised to learn that the Australian lifestyle then was very similar to what ours in the United States was at that time. So we quickly realized that we had made a good decision to enter the Australian market.

Immediately upon arriving
at the airport in Australia,
Sid could tell there was a great need for
a comprehensive weight-loss program . . .
there were a lot of overweight people.

Moreover, the Australian Health Department had just published statistics on how much money obesity-related diseases were costing the country. Because of socialized medicine, a doctor was not allowed to treat a patient with prevention methods. And doctors were limited as to how many office visits a patient could make and how often for the same medical condition. There was much talk in the media about this financial drain on the Health Department. So in addition to fulfilling a need, the timing was right for the introduction of our program.

We did face some competition from the Weight Watchers franchise, which was doing about $4 million annually when we arrived, but we soon passed them up like a freight train. We bought out our partner's 10 percent interest in the company, and we went to work.

Sid has often said that our partner made a lasting contribution to our Australian operation by recruiting Harry Mowson. Harry was to play a major role in our success there and beyond, because Harry could get things done. He later told me that at that time he thought ours was an American company trying to lose money as a write-off for tax purposes. Harry was thrilled when Sid finally arrived and they began to accomplish things.

Positive things began to happen. Harry was happy to learn that we were genuinely trying to develop a credible program that would greatly benefit the Australian people and return a profit in the process. Sid and Harry busied themselves scouting out locations for the nine centers we planned to open. I, in turn, was up to my neck writing training manuals that we needed for the first training class.

Choosing a Name for Our New Company

Sid suggested we name the company "Jenny Craig" because of the public relations benefits. He felt that using my name would establish an identity better than a name like "Weight Loss, Inc." After all, with the name Jenny Craig, customers can identify with a *person*. Even Gloria Marshall salons were named after Gloria Bergendahl, with her maiden name. For a woman's business, I think it's good to have a female at the head of the company. Because I was going to be the spokesperson, using my name also helped identify me with my market.

> For a woman's business,
> I think it's good to have a female
> at the head of the company.

We did do some market research regarding other possible names. We considered Ultra System (because of the success of NutriSystem). And we considered Figure Magic. We had about 10 names, all of which would have been appropriate. But it was always my name that people we asked responded to, because they felt they were dealing with a person rather than a corporation. The official name, when we first started, was Jenny Craig Weight Loss, Inc., and the centers were called Jenny Craig Weight Loss Centres, though the company name got shortened later, after we were better known.

I was something of an anomaly, running a business in Australia, where there were very few women-owned businesses in those days.

There were times when I was totally ignored: Businesspeople we worked with directed all their communication to Sid. There was a male chauvinist mentality in business in Australia at that time. For example, while advertising plans were being discussed in a meeting, the men there just sort of ignored me and talked around me. Their comments were directed toward Sid even though my name was on the door. Thankfully, once they discovered that I had something to contribute to their ideas and my veto carried weight, they began to elicit my opinions.

But overall, I think many women admired the fact that I was in business and was successful. I think it even opened doors to more women going into business for themselves. Many of the women I met were shy and not very assertive—primarily because women didn't work in business, so they just weren't accustomed to dealing with businesspeople or professionals in an assertive way. This is one of the reasons I conducted classes on assertiveness at the centers.

Today, of course, it's not at all unusual to see women in top executive positions in Australian companies, but when we were there, I can't recall one, except perhaps at companies publishing women's magazines. But in corporations and public companies, there weren't a lot of women in power.

My whole life, I've done everything I could to promote women's advancement and growth, both in business and in my private life.

Building Our Management Team

After settling in, the next thing we did was to find the most credible doctor, psychologist, and dietitian in Australia who would help us design the program according to the Australian guidelines and health needs. We needed someone who understood the psychology of weight loss, because weight management relies on behavior modification. And we needed someone with credibility, so we went

to Royal Melbourne University and simply asked who was the doctor in charge of clinical psychology, and they directed us to Dr. Ian
Campbell. We told him what our concept was, showed brochures,
and explained what we were trying to accomplish, and he was very
interested in working with us.

> # We needed someone who understood
> # the psychology of weight loss,
> # because weight management
> # relies on behavior modification.

Then we asked who was head of the medical division of the
Victorian Medical Association, and we found Dr. George Santoro,
who knew many of the doctors in Australia. We wanted doctors to
understand what our program was, so they would possibly refer patients to us. Dr. Santoro is still with us today. Then we ran an ad in
the newspaper for a nutritionist, and we found Ruth Meier, who
had many years of experience teaching classes on health and nutrition at a university in Melbourne.

Hiring Counselors for Our New Weight Loss Centers

Almost 300 women responded to our ad for counselors, program
directors, and managers in the local newspaper in Melbourne. We
expected to hire about 100 employees to staff the centers that were
opening. Lorrie Blizzard, who had previously worked for me as a
supervisor at Gloria Marshall while I was in Chicago, had also
moved to Australia to work for us. She had called me before I left
for Australia, saying she was still at Body Contour, Inc., but wasn't
happy after NutriSystem took over. Since we were going to Aus-

tralia to open a new business, she wondered if I would keep her in mind if we needed any help. As a supervisor, she knew how to train employees. So when I realized I needed help interviewing and training, I contacted Lorrie Blizzard and she joined us in Australia.

My daughter Michelle, who was 24 years old at the time, also helped me out. Michelle had attended college for three years and then went to work in the Gloria Marshall salons/Body Contour centers, so she also knew the business. She knew sales and understood the whole concept of weight loss; she had become a manager working in several Gloria Marshall centers. I figured she would be ideal. She came to Australia to visit and to see what we were doing, and she decided to stay on.

Lorrie, Michelle, and I interviewed all those women in our apartment because the centers were still under construction. We turned the living room, the dining room, and a small spare bedroom into offices with desks and chairs. Our apartment was the penthouse suite, so the elevator went directly up to our living room. We had to have the applicants sit downstairs in the lobby on a couch we had brought in. They would complete their application forms as they waited. As each applicant came down the elevator after her interview, a helper was there to send another applicant up.

One of the funniest things happened that week. One day, I looked out my window and saw that men were hanging out of every window in the government office building across the street. Some had binoculars looking at the women pouring in and out of our building. Our ad had requested "trim, attractive women with high energy" (which we were allowed to request back in 1982), so most of the applicants were above-average looking. You can imagine what those men were thinking!

That same day, our landlord came sneaking up the back stairs and used his key to enter the apartment. He looked around quizzically as we told him why we had to use the apartment for interviewing. Once he saw there was no hanky-panky, he wished us well and went on his way. We still laugh about that incident.

Getting Accustomed to Cultural Differences

After interviewing all the applicants, we hired 100 of them. We knew we'd lose about 20 percent before opening or shortly there-after, so we allowed for that attrition. We scheduled our first train-ing class to be held in the Victorian Economic Council (VEC) building. Our training classroom was arranged theater style, with a stage at the front of the room. Humorous things happened during our two weeks of training.

We were new to the Australian culture, so we hadn't yet learned the vernacular or colloquialisms. My style of training has always been one of role-playing. I've found people learn best when they see the way it should be done and then experience it from the buyer's as well as from the seller's viewpoint.

The first unusual thing to happen occurred on the very first day. Sid opened the training class by telling everyone why we were there and what it would mean to fellow Australians, who up until then had little or no help in dealing with the serious problem of obesity, which was prominent throughout their country. He then proceeded to give me this big buildup, expecting a standing ova-tion type of response as I was introduced. When his speech built to a crescendo and I went up on stage, no one even applauded: There was dead silence. Sid began clapping vigorously and managed to get a soft applause from the audience.

I later learned that Australian women were shy and not sure what the protocol was in the world of business. I've since seen an enormous change in that respect over the past 20 years.

I made other blunders. After the first week of training, I invited Dr. Campbell to sit in on our training class to see firsthand what we were all about. I began to call on people to demonstrate a typical presentation that a client would receive when coming to a center. After a complete presentation, I called on one of the students (Jane), a former nurse. She stood up and I asked her, "What would you say if a client walked in and said she only wanted to lose a couple of inches in her fanny?"

Jane's face turned beet red, her eyes filled with tears, and she sat down without answering. The whole class exploded in laughter. Needless to say, I was confused—until Dr. Campbell called me aside and explained that *fanny* in Australia referred to the female genitals; they call the rear end a *bum*. I've been teased about that faux pas over the years.

I'm glad there were some laughs, because we were all working very hard. Having so much work to do in preparing handouts for the class, I had to be at the stenographer's office at 5:30 A.M. every morning to dictate the information and run off copies. I was then able to arrive before 9:00 A.M. at the training class fully prepared. I received raves on how well presented all the training material was. I'm sure everyone thought I had done all that long before the first day of training. But the truth is that I was barely one step ahead of each day's training material! I was also writing behavior education classes until late at night to be used once the centers were open. Those were very long days.

Opening Day in Melbourne

In early May 1983, we opened nine centers in Melbourne. People have asked me why we chose Melbourne rather than Sydney for our first centers. Perhaps the main reason was that the food companies that produced our food were located there. We were continually developing new foods, so logistically it was a better choice. Also, our attorney who advised us on Australian labor laws had his office there. Adding to that, we fell in love with Melbourne and its people. Knowing what I know now, I would still choose to live there.

Melbourne has always reminded me of America back in the 1950s: friendly neighbors offering support whenever it's needed. We quickly developed cherished friendships that have given us much joy over the years, not the least of which is our 20-year relationship with Harry Mowson.

Harry came to us as a sort of real estate expert. He knew his way around Melbourne, and he was a whiz at breaking through the cobwebs to get things done. Harry would taxi over signed leases to the property owners to expedite our openings. We began to refer to him as "Harry Houdini" because he could sometimes accomplish the impossible. Even though he is now a successful Jenny Craig franchisee, there's still strong belief throughout the company-owned center staff that if you want to get something done, give it to Harry. There aren't enough accolades to describe Harry and his contribution to our beginnings in Australia.

Despite all our hard work back then (it was not unusual for me to have 15- to 18-hour workdays), we had fun, too. Some weekends, we would have parties on the veranda of our apartment with our whole staff attending. Let me tell you, Australians know how to party. It's a wonder we weren't evicted from the building because of the racket we made. We would have a disc jockey come in and play loud music to dance to. With 100 plus people dancing, I'm sure there were times the building shook under the strain. Believe me, we had very tolerant neighbors; they were not unlike most Australians, who understand and favorably respond to the word *party*.

It was a great time for us; we were watching our company grow from strength to strength and it was a great time to be in Australia. Yes, there were fun times, but most of the fun was at work. I have always believed that whatever career one chooses, if it isn't fun, they've made the wrong choice.

Early Challenges—And How We Overcame Them

It wasn't all fun and games. During our very first week in business, we encountered a potential catastrophe. Sid got a call from the Australian Health Department director. She had noticed that our vitamins were in small packets of a daily supply. They had been developed and packaged by a U.S. vitamin company. We had incorporated selenium in the mix because our U.S. vitamin company had suggested it, since the Australian soil did not contain selenium. And some research has shown selenium to be helpful in the prevention of cancer. So it was with that in mind that we told them to add it to our mix.

The director told Sid that we couldn't mix the vitamins together in packets. Sid replied that since the vitamins get mixed together once they are ingested, what was the reason for not allowing them to be packaged together? She didn't appreciate his attempt at humor. She then told him that selenium could be distributed only by a chemist (that is, a pharmacist), so if we proceeded to distribute those vitamins in our centers, she would close them down—just as we were getting ready to open!

Initially, we were devastated. We had invested so much, and we had scheduled advertising due to hit the public that Monday morning. We couldn't believe the Health Department director had waited to notify us until just a few days before we were supposed to open. She called right before the weekend, a time when there would be nothing we could do to rectify the situation anyway.

In her defense, she probably hadn't known earlier about the opening, but when we started to run the teaser ads about "Jenny Craig is coming . . ." there was a lot of talk about our company, which I suppose prompted the Health Department to check in to see what we were doing. All we could think about was the advertising that would run and the centers that wouldn't be open for business.

She gave us two options: Return the vitamin packets to the United States or dump them overboard. We chose the latter, because it would have cost an additional $1,700 to return them to the manufacturer. (We like believing that we are responsible for providing healthier fish.)

Because our label was on the packaging, the vitamins would have been useless in the United States. We knew we would not have centers there for at least two years. We ate the cost of all those vitamins and had the expense of developing new ones that complied with the Health Department guidelines. The episode proved to be a costly mistake, but far less costly than the alternative of not opening at all.

Then Ruth Meier, our nutritionist, told us we had made another mistake. We had developed single-serving packages of pancake mix as a breakfast selection. Ruth said that Australians didn't eat pancakes for breakfast. She said Australians ate toast with Vegemite spread on it. I didn't know what Vegemite was: I had never heard of it. But after tasting that stuff, I reasoned that "if the Aussies will eat that, they'll have to *love* pancakes." We had only three products as options for breakfast in the beginning, so we needed pancakes as one of them; besides, we had spent a lot of money developing and producing the product. Well, pancakes turned out to be our best-selling product. We learned a valuable lesson that sometimes necessity overrides conventional wisdom, and when in doubt, go with your gut.

> We learned a valuable lesson
> that sometimes necessity
> overrides conventional wisdom,
> and when in doubt, go with your gut.

Also, I can't say we were an immediate success after opening the first centers. Our ad agency had run some teasers on TV and in the main newspaper. The first ads said, *"Jenny Craig is coming to town."* The next ad said, *"Jenny Craig is coming to town and she may take it* off." Then they ran an ad that said, *"Jenny Craig is coming to town and she may take it* all *off."* Those were pretty provocative words on television, and everyone was talking about them. Bear in mind that no one knew who Jenny Craig was. We heard announcers saying things like, "Who do you think she is?" and "Where do you think she'll take it off?"

Unfortunately, I think once we ran our grand opening ad, many of the calls we got were inquisitive callers wanting to know what we were all about, so they were not necessarily prospective customers. We continued to get a lot of calls, but with inexperienced people staffing the centers, a lot of the calls were lost. I was traveling around to the centers trying to do some additional training, but everyone was so busy, there wasn't much time to train them.

I would conduct the consultations and have different staff members sit in with me so that they'd learn how to answer intelligently any question that might arise. Gradually, with the help of Dr. Campbell, we developed a staff of knowledgeable, enthusiastic people dedicated to the work of making each and every client successful.

Another challenge I believe we faced was the attitude of Australian women in general. In Australia, most of our clients were homemakers, though the ages ranged from 30 years old to 55 years old. Regardless of age, though, they seemed to lack confidence and assertiveness. I first noticed this because, in addition to writing the manuals and behavior education classes, I worked in the centers in different roles: some days as counselor, some days as receptionist or program director; occasionally, I held the behavior education classes. I can remember one evening in particular when I held a class on "being assertive."

Learning to be assertive is a necessary component if one is to take charge of his or her eating behavior. You must learn how to say "no" when offered food that is not part of your healthy eating plan. The trick is to learn how to do it without offending the person offering it.

Learning to be assertive is a necessary component if one is to take charge of his or her eating behavior.

In that class, we usually give examples and ask the clients what their response would be, and then guide them as we go along. Because our clientele consisted of 85 percent women, most of the attendees were female; in fact, I don't remember seeing one male in that class.

During that particular class I called on one of the women and asked, "What would you say if your cousin borrowed money promising to pay you back in a week and three months had gone by without his doing so?" She looked at me and meekly said, "Nothing." This wasn't the response I was looking for. So I had her repeat after me, "Cousin, when you asked me for the money, I didn't hesitate to help you because I trusted you and believed you would live up to your word to return it in a week. I really need that money, so how soon can you get it to me?"

Then I called on another woman and asked, "Suppose your doctor gave you an appointment and you were sitting in his reception room for over an hour past the time of your appointment. What would you say to him?" Again the answer was a soft-spoken "Nothing." So I gave her the dialogue that would be appropriate, something like, "Doctor, I know how busy you are, and I, too, am very busy. That's why I made an appointment instead of just showing up at your office. What can we do to make sure this never happens again?"

With each consecutive question, I could see the clients were gaining a little more confidence. As the class ended and they were filing out, there was a slightly militant air about them. I knew right then and there that 35 men were going to be blessing me that night for giving their wives the confidence to take control of their eating habits.

As I've already pointed out, I was surprised to find how shy many Australian women were in those days. Because most women never worked outside the home, they were not accustomed to calling the shots. Assertiveness was not a part of their demeanor.

The Beginning of Our Success in Australia

Perhaps the real turning point for us was when Sid was able to get me on a national TV program called *New Faces*. It was the most popular show in Australia, with ratings similar to *The Tonight Show* when Johnny Carson hosted it. It was on the *New Faces* show that Paul Hogan (Crocodile Dundee) was discovered. The show was live on Sunday evenings, and I would go on to do a 60-second live commercial. Before long, the host and I began to banter back and forth, and the commercials ended up running for two full minutes and sometimes even more. Soon we were getting more phone calls than we could handle.

Before we opened centers in Adelaide, each week the host would ask me, "Jenny, when are you going to open in Adelaide? Those people need you, too." This same question came up every week for several weeks. Finally, one Sunday I announced that Adelaide was opening the following day. The band gave a drum roll, and there was whooping and hollering in the studio.

When we opened our doors in Adelaide on Monday, there was

a line of people a block long waiting to get in. We had to issue numbers to the people because even with about 20 employees working, we couldn't get to them right away. Adelaide set a precedent as to what a grand opening should be. We continued to expand throughout Australia, opening more than 50 centers within a year, which must have been some kind of record.

And we knew we were successful when we became a household name. For example, at one televised cricket match, the cameras panning the crowd picked up a sign aimed at the overweight captain of the English team: "See Jenny Craig. Quick." We had a good laugh over that one.

Working Successfully with Family

Our company was an equal partnership for Sid and me, because our business was marketing driven. Sid was such a brilliant and creative marketing genius; he was just as important as the field work, which I handled. We had complementary skills and talents, and I think that's what makes a family business—or any business—work. As a very smart person once said, if two people agree on everything, then one of them isn't necessary. And I think that's also true with skills: If business partners have exactly the same skills, then one of them isn't necessary, except as a helper or investor.

Who can say how my life would have been different if I hadn't met Sid? I think I would have been successful, but maybe not to the extent we've been successful together.

In addition to working with my husband, I was helped by my daughters. Both Michelle and Denise had come to work with us in Australia. Denise had attended the University of Indiana at Bloomington, where she majored in French, and she went to the Sorbonne for her last year. After college, she worked for Gucci and other companies. Like Michelle, she came to visit us in Australia and decided to stay. We never really sat down and said, "How would you like to work here?" Both my daughters just started helping me out and sort of fell into staying with the business.

In fact, both Sid and I thought our kids would go off and do other things, but four out of five of our kids have worked with us in the business. Both Susan and Steven worked summers for us while they were in college: Susan was in sales, and Steven worked stacking foods in the food rooms at the centers. When we came back to the United States, we gave Denise a franchise in Bakersfield, and from there, she opened Fresno.

By that time, Steven and Susan had graduated from college, and they opened a franchise in Tampa, Florida. Steven had graduated with a major in business, so we felt that he could be a great help to Susan, whose strengths were in sales and training. Together they were quite a team.

I liked the fact that our kids were not only motivated to be in the business but that they were *good* at it. For example, one day I was running a little late, so I asked Michelle if she would get a class started while I went to pick up the printed training material. She said, "Oh, Mom, I don't think I can do it." I assured her she could, because she was familiar with the material and how to present it. I stayed around only long enough to see her neck break out in red blotches as her trembling voice delivered the instructions for the practice session.

But when I returned two hours later, Michelle was up on the stage singing into the mike. It hadn't taken her long to adjust to performing in public. From then on, she proved to be a good public speaker. That's a good example of how exposing yourself to what you fear is the best way to conquer it.

The only disadvantage to so many of us working together occurred when we would all get together at Christmas or during summers: Instead of talking about family things, our get-togethers invariably turned into business meetings. Of course, our kids didn't always agree with some of the things that *we* wanted to do, and sometimes there were discussions about our differences of opinion.

I'd like to say something about my relationship with Sid's children. I have never considered them stepchildren. To me they are *my* children. I love them in the same way I love the children I gave birth to. I believe they feel the same way about me. If not, it doesn't show. When people ask me how many children I have, I always answer "five" because in my heart I have five children, no matter how they began life.

I think some families can work really well together in business—we all did—but other families can't do that; it depends on the dynamics of the group. I think whatever the family business is, it's important that *each* individual needs to feel that he or she is making a valuable contribution to the benefit of the whole company, because many times one or two family members will try to take over.

> I think whatever the family business is,
> it's important that *each* individual
> needs to feel he or she is
> making a valuable contribution
> to the benefit of the whole company.

A franchise is an ideal situation; Michelle had her own, Denise had hers, and Susan and Steven had theirs. In a sense, though, they were competing with each other. They competed as business-people, but if one did better than the other, their success didn't affect their personal relationships. I think this would have been different if they were all working in a corporate office, where some kind of competition and dissension would build, and there might be a difficult division of responsibility. They would probably also vie for who would take over the business.

For two years, we devoted our full-time attention to opening centers and developing staff so that one day we could return to the United States. I cannot emphasize enough the importance of training and grooming people for higher positions if a company is to grow and succeed.

> # I cannot emphasize enough
> # the importance of training
> # and grooming people for higher positions
> # if a company is to grow and succeed.

Obviously, we spent a lot of time building our business. So when people ask me what places I've seen in Australia, they're usually surprised to learn that the only places we visited were places where we were planning to open centers. We didn't take a vacation for two years. Finally we took a trip to Perth to close a deal for a franchise in Western Australia, and from there we went to Hong Kong for three days. In Hong Kong we surveyed the area for any potential viability for Jenny Craig centers. So even our vacations were motivated with business in mind.

Shortly before we were to open in Sydney, Michelle called to say that she was about to get married in Chicago. She had met her fiancé, Duayne Weinger, when she was still working for Body Contour, Inc., in Chicago, and they continued their relationship even after she moved to Australia. She had gotten engaged when they met for a vacation in Hawaii. Michelle, of course, wanted me to attend the wedding, but, sadly, I had to decline. I was in the middle of a training class, and I just couldn't leave. I promised her a celebration when she came back to Australia and apologized for not being able to make her wedding. Had she given me some advance notice, I could have worked my schedule around it. She told me it was a spontaneous decision, and because her fiancé Duayne's parents lived in Chicago, they would be there for the small family wedding.

After their wedding, she and Duayne came to Australia and together they opened the Brisbane centers. They both worked very hard, and soon they were both hooked on the business. They were a tremendous help in the growth of our Australian operation.

Soon after they arrived, I gave Michelle a bridal shower and a wedding party at one of the best restaurants in Sydney. Most of the people attending were employees, but they were all friends who knew Michelle from our early days in Melbourne. Actually, Michelle had three wedding celebrations because before returning to Australia, she went to New Orleans and her dad had a party in honor of their wedding.

I am thankful that Denise had decided to join us in Australia. Before long, she became the national trainer and traveled throughout Australia giving initial training and follow-up training classes. She was invaluable to our growth and success there. That experience also prepared her for the role she would play later on as a franchisee of Jenny Craig.

All of our kids joined us in the business because they were truly inspired by what we were doing. Imagine a business that is financially successful because it helps people to improve not only their looks, but their health—a business that rewards you with visual proof of its efficacy and fills you with pride as you listen to the *life-changing stories* of clients, every day. If you can imagine such a company, you will understand how easy it is to fall in love with the concept and look forward with anticipation to each workday. That's what the Jenny Craig program is all about. Those are the rewards that spurred us on to work harder, longer, and to be more determined than ever to make every client a success story.

Imagine a business that is financially successful
because it helps people to improve
not only their looks, but their health
—a business that rewards you with visual
proof of its efficacy and fills you
with pride as you listen to
the *life-changing stories* of clients, every day.

The Philosophy behind the Jenny Craig Program

I feel I would be remiss if I didn't talk a little about what the Jenny Craig philosophy is as well as what has become my own personal philosophy for a well-balanced and healthful lifestyle. Since 1983, the program has evolved into something quite different from its beginning.

When we first started out, in 1982 in Australia, most of our clients were homemakers, ranging in age from 30 years old to 55 years old. Since then, of course, the demographic profile of our clients has changed, though we still have primarily women clients: Eight-five percent are female. It's still a broad age range for us, probably even broader because of the number of children we have in the program (tweens and teenagers, mostly; we have a requirement that children must be at least 13 years old to start our program).

Today, if you were to find the average of our client base, it would be a woman around 40 years old and 30 to 40 pounds overweight. But that's just a mean: There are many clients who are younger and have less weight to lose, while some are younger with more weight to lose. Similarly, we have older clients who have less weight to lose and older clients who have more weight to lose. In addition, the socioeconomics of our clients have changed over the years: Approximately 70 percent of our clients now work outside the home, whereas 20 years ago that wasn't true.

We have, from time to time, changed some things and added things in order to keep up with the changing needs of the consumer. We have incorporated changes that resulted from up-to-the-minute research in order to give the clients a greater chance for successful weight management.

But the one thing that has never changed is our basic philosophy. Maintaining a healthy body weight and living a balanced lifestyle should not be approached with an all-or-nothing attitude. My many years of experience in watching scores of successful lifestyle changes in people have taught me that *moderation* is the key to success. None of us are perfect and therefore we will not always behave perfectly. That's okay: We don't have to behave perfectly in order to achieve the goals we set for ourselves.

Maintaining a healthy body weight and living a balanced lifestyle should not be approached with an all-or-nothing attitude.

I've seen countless examples of people who allow one slipup to sabotage their good intentions. We, as humans, will make mistakes. We seem to accept that in most areas of our daily life, except where diet is concerned. If we fall off our intended eating program, many of us chastise ourselves with self-talk like, "I blew it . . . I can't do this," or "I failed again . . . I knew that would happen." That kind of self-talk is destructive to present as well as future attempts at lifestyle change.

Weight management is just what the term implies: the ability to manage one's body weight. Management is an ongoing process and is not accomplished in one single act no matter how sincere the effort. Think of this way: When you go to your hairstylist for a haircut, do you then expect it to last a lifetime? When you go to your dentist to have your teeth cleaned, do you then expect that you will never again have to do that? Of course not; that is all part of *body maintenance*. Why, then, should we expect any success at weight loss to be a one-time procedure?

Weight management is an ongoing process that requires monitoring, assessment, and lifestyle adjustment, as required by the indicators just like all other acts of body health management. Just as a toothache is a signal that something is wrong and needs attention, so are your scales a detector of the need for a lifestyle adjustment. We are all creatures of habit. Habits are nothing more than *practiced behaviors*. The longer you practice a behavior, the longer it takes to change it. If you're a tennis player or a golfer, you understand that it takes effort to correct any motion that is causing you to underperform your ability. Similarly, when you are making health-enhancing lifestyle changes, you must give time to the new behaviors in order for them to become habits or practiced behaviors.

There are many different reasons why people gain weight and came to us: Some women, like me, gained weight during pregnancy. One client wrote the following letter to us, describing her situation:

> I gained 70 pounds when I was pregnant with my son. Unable to lose the extra weight after childbirth, I felt ugly and had very low self-esteem. I eventually managed to lose 30 pounds on my own, but found that the rest of my excess weight just wouldn't come off. That's when I decided to go to Jenny Craig. I lost the 30 pounds I couldn't take off on my own, and have maintained my weight for three years. I truly believe in this program. As a mat-

ter of fact, I'm now a manager of a Jenny Craig Centre, where I help motivate new clients who are as unhappy with themselves as I once was.

In addition, professional women often eat on the run, grabbing fast food, which becomes the norm for them to eat. Other women go through injury or extended illness, so they gain weight because they're sedentary. Emotional reasons, such as a death in the family, or marriage, are other reasons. You'd be surprised how many people—especially women—gain weight after they get married, either because they're fixing meals for their husband or preparing more food than they used to. And women who have children often finish their kids' dinners because they don't want to throw out the food.

We have seen such a cross-section of people with the whole spectrum of reasons why people gain weight. We understand the stress and challenges that women face. And now, because our population is aging, some women will be gaining weight during menopause on account of hormone replacement therapy, which, any doctor will tell you, adds weight. It might not be much, maybe only 5 pounds, but if you've gained another 5 pounds on your own, that's an added 10 pounds, and then you may gain more from there.

I believe the reason many people fail at weight maintenance is because of their expectations. They set unrealistic goals and view the journey the same way we think of a train ride. That is, they set a destination, and when the destination is in view or has been achieved, their job is over, mission accomplished. Common sense will tell you that if you've been practicing certain behaviors for many years, you shouldn't expect to change those behaviors in a couple of months with a one-time effort. So then, lifestyle changes that enhance your health and improve the appearance of your body are not something you go *on and off* in the same way you get on and off a train or a bus. To be successful over the long term requires vigilance and practice.

> I believe the reason many people
> fail at weight maintenance is
> because . . . they set unrealistic goals.

Success also requires a paradigm shift. When someone tells me they would like to lose weight, my first question is "why?" If they answer with anything other than "because I want to change my lifestyle so that I can look better, feel better, and improve my health for the rest of my life," I explain that they should expect to achieve short-term results.

And there's nothing wrong with wanting only short-term results. Some people have an upcoming event that they are preparing for, and that's fine. But you've probably heard it said when planning to make an investment in the stock market, "Short-term investment produces short-term results." If you are seriously considering changing your lifestyle for long-term results, it's important that you know what to expect.

When trying to change a behavior, it helps to envision a grandfather clock with a hanging pendulum. When the pendulum has swung to one side, we all know it has to swing to the other side before it can come back to the middle. The same is true when trying to break a habit. Again, if you've ever played golf or tennis, then you know it takes patience and commitment to change a habit that is counterproductive to your game. In the beginning it feels different, but the longer you practice the new behavior, the easier it becomes until you can do it without a lot of thought. Eventually, you reach the point that your new behavior is automatic. Maintaining your success then will be relatively easy. Arriving at that point takes patience and commitment. This is what we mean when we say it takes "skill power," not willpower. It's knowing what to do and doing it.

I've seen some terrific success stories. One of the earliest successes that impressed me happened at my Healthletic gym. One of our clients was a woman in her sixties. She didn't have a lot of weight to lose, but you know how your skin gets lax after a certain age. She wanted to lose a little weight, but primarily she wanted to tone her body.

One day, she came in with a whole new hairdo—it was all swept up, and she looked terrific. I mentioned to her that she looked so different, to which she replied, "Don't I look younger? This is my way of having a nonsurgical facelift!" What a great attitude.

Another great success story I remember is from the early 1970s when I was working at the Gloria Marshall Figure Salons, in the Metairie center in New Orleans. One day, one of my clients came into the salon carrying a box wrapped in gift paper. She had lost about 35 pounds over six months, and we were very proud of her success. I wondered what she was bringing; I thought maybe it was a gift for me.

But when she opened the box, she said, "I just wanted to show you this because it's something I have always wanted, and my husband gave it to me last night as an anniversary gift." It was a black negligee. She said, "This is the first time I felt like I could put it on." Well, I started crying, because I'd seen all the dedication she had put into achieving this goal.

Other clients had a great sense of humor about their weight loss. One time, in Australia, I was making a commercial with a client, a young man who had lost more than 200 pounds. We were filming in a park, and as the two of us sat down on a bench, he sat about three feet to my right. So I said to him, "You know, the camera isn't going to be able to capture both of us this far apart; you need to come closer to me." He smiled and said, "I'm sorry, my mind still hasn't registered that I'm smaller."

After we finished filming, I asked him what the biggest adjustment was that he had to make in his life. And he said, "I can't get used to women talking to me and being aggressive." I told him, "Well, I'm sure you'll get used to that quickly!" And I wished him good luck.

One of the most moving stories I recall, though, happened during our early years of Jenny Craig, Inc., in our Santa Monica center in California, shortly after we moved back to the United States in 1985. This gal came in with her mother, who had lost about 50 pounds over six months or so. As her mother was going in to get her consultation, she said to me, "You know, I never realized how beautiful my mother was before." It's stories like these that make my work exciting and fulfilling.

And clients continue to write in to us to tell their own stories. For example, one of our male clients wrote the following letter:

> As an endocrinologist specializing in diabetes, I know how excess weight can adversely affect health. Most of my patients are overweight, and it's part of my job to put them on a diet. But, at 250 pounds, I was a good teacher, but a bad example.
>
> Jenny Craig changed that. Now that I've lost 55 pounds, I feel good, have more stamina, and am involved in outdoor sports which I was unable to participate in because of my weight—mountain climbing, boogie boarding, and surfing. Now, when I tell my patients to lose weight, I recommend Jenny Craig.

Striving for a Balanced Life

If you think of your life as a diagram of a wheel with spokes or segments representing each area of your lifestyle, then it's easy to understand why balance is so important. If the segments consist of family, career, health, spiritual, and love, then we need to periodically assess how we're doing in each of those areas. Knowing that a wheel doesn't turn unless it's round and balanced, so is it true that our life isn't harmonious unless each area of our existence is also rounded and balanced.

When one segment is out of balance, it affects all other areas of our lives in much the same way a wheel that is out of balance will make the journey bumpy. Sometimes, we become so focused on one segment of our lives that we neglect all the other areas that are also important to our happiness as well as to our feelings of accomplishment and fulfillment.

It's helpful to sit down in a quiet place once a month, list these categories, and ask yourself four questions relative to each spoke of your life wheel:

1. How am I doing on a scale of 1 to 10?
2. What can I do to make it better?
3. What do I need to do to accomplish my goal of a 10?
4. How soon can I start?

Once you have assessed where you are in relation to your goal, the next step is to map out a strategy for change in order to accomplish your goals. Most of us go through life without giving thought to how closely our life resembles the kind of life we want and dream about for ourselves, as well as for our families. We allow each day to pass with only the immediate needs or crises dictating to us how we spend that day, instead of planning a long-term goal with a day-to-day strategy for achieving that goal. You will always have detours or interruptions in your daily life, but if you concentrate on doing the *important* rather than the *immediate*, you can accomplish a lot more.

If you concentrate on doing the *important*
rather than the *immediate*,
you can accomplish a lot more.

Wrapping Up in Australia

By the end of the summer of 1985, our two-year noncompete contract was coming to an end, and we decided to return to
the United States. I continue to be amazed at the extent of
my recognition when I walked down the street in Australia during
the two years we were there. One Sunday Sid, Jim McCormick,
and I had gone to breakfast at a little neighborhood restaurant. As
we entered, practically everyone in the place said, "Hello, Jenny!"

As we left the restaurant, kids were riding by on bikes and
yelling, "Hey, Jenny!" while giving me a thumbs-up. Finally, Jim
said he was thinking about crossing the street because it was getting to be embarrassing for him, because no one was calling, "Hey,
Jim!" (Of course, he was just joking.) I have always felt indebted to
the Australian people for their warm acceptance of me along with
their enthusiasm and support for the Jenny Craig company. Each
time I visit there, I truly feel at home.

We tried to give back to the community as a way of expressing
our appreciation. While we were there, we teamed up with ANZ
Bank to be the main sponsors of the Australian Olympic Team. We
also bought a new canoe for the Olympic rowing team so that they
would have a better chance at winning. We opened five safe houses
across the country for battered women and children along with
many other contributions too numerous to name. I treasure the experiences we shared during the two years we were there. Sid agrees
that those were two of the most exciting and happiest years of our
life together. But it was time to go home.

I was born in this little house, in Berwick, Louisiana, a small town about 100 miles south of New Orleans. I lived here only until I was 1 year old; in 1933, we moved to New Orleans.

My mother, Gertrude Acosta Guidroz, shown here in 1938, at age 37; I was 6 when this picture was taken. Whenever I think of my mother, I'm reminded what a kind, generous woman she was, devoting her whole life to her family.

This photo was taken on Thanksgiving in the early 1980s. My sister Trudy (*left*), my dad (at age 86), and my sister Elsie spent the holiday at the home of Trudy's daughter in New Orleans.

During my senior year of high school I worked at an upscale department store called Godchaux's. I was persuaded to enter the beauty pageant at the company picnic—and I won! Here I am, on the day of the pageant in 1950, in a local park with the boy I was dating at the time, Ralph Bourgeois.

I was only 22 years old the day I married Bobby Bourcq—exactly: It was my birthday, August 7, 1954. This picture was taken at my sister-in-law's parents' house, a beautiful antebellum home that was so big that the whole bridal party got ready there. The marriage ceremony took place in a little church, and we were married for 21 years.

One of the highlights of my work with Home Decorators was attending the company's annual awards banquet. We had earned the trip because we had done the best in the country. We were shown how silverware and our other products were made. This picture, taken in the company's rose garden after a luncheon in Newark, New York, in 1956, shows (*left to right*), Anita Landry, me, my sister Elsie, and Adele Digby, who later became my partner when we opened our own gym, Healthletic.

After I sold my gym, I went to work for Body Contour, Inc., in the company's Gloria Marshall Figure Salons. Body Contour held annual conventions for salon supervisors from all areas. Gloria Bergendahl, who started the company with her husband, Alan, is sixth from the left; I'm third from the right; and on the far right is Lorrie Blizzard, who came to Australia later to work with Sid and me when we started Jenny Craig, Inc.

Healthletic was the first business I owned;
it was a gym that I started with
my friend Adele Digby.

Sid and I were married in Las Vegas, at Caesars Palace, on February 18, 1979. It was a small ceremony because it was a second marriage for both of us. We were very much in love, and we've had 25 happy years together so far!

Jenny Craig, Inc., has been a great success for Sid and me: For our first wedding anniversary, in 1980, Sid gave me this beautiful Clinet (*center*). This photo was taken at our Downey, California, home, with my daughter Denise (*left*), Sid, and my daughter Michelle.

Here I am *(center)*, with some staff members in 1983. Although my visits to the centers usually involved training the managers and counselors, while there I would do whatever was needed: answering the phones, enrolling clients, explaining menus to clients, even packaging food bags when it was necessary.

This is one of the original nine Jenny Craig Weight Loss Centres that we opened in Melbourne, Australia, in May 1983. We located these centers in strip malls, to offer some measure of privacy to our clients—they could drive right up and go in.

This is me in 1983, when I was the company spokesperson for all our advertising in Australia. We used me in ads because nobody knew yet who or what Jenny Craig was!

One of our first celebrity spokespeople when we opened Jenny Craig, Inc., in the United States was Elliott Gould, shown here with Sid and me in 1986 or 1987. We had always used celebrities in our advertising in all our businesses; in addition to working with Elliott, Cindy Williams, of *Laverne & Shirley* fame, and Jerry Mathers, of *Leave It to Beaver*, did commercials, talking about their weight loss on the Jenny Craig program.

I've been fortunate to meet some very famous people in my life. I met Paul Newman at a charity function in 1993. While I was in New York promoting one of my cookbooks, which he was kind enough to endorse, I was thrilled at the opportunity to have lunch with him. In my day he was *the hunk*, and as you can see...he still is!

Sid and I were thrilled when Jenny Craig, Inc., went public in 1992. Here we are at the New York Stock Exchange, looking up from the floor of the Exchange as our company name appeared in lights. There are no words to describe the excitement of that experience.

Since the mid-1970s, Sid and I have owned thoroughbred racehorses. Here we are in the winner's circle, along with our trainer, Hal King (*far right*), and co-owner, Gene Victor (*fourth to left of me in rear*). Gene is a college basketball coach and has been a friend for more than 20 years.

Opening day in 1994 at the Del Mar Race Track. I'm known for my hats; in fact, I've been one of the judges of the Best Hat Contest at the races since 1989 or so until a couple of years ago, when Sid and I had horses running and it was difficult to leave to judge the contest. On opening day all the women wear hats, and there's a contest for the prettiest, the most original, the one that best portrays the horse theme, and the funniest. I've loved hats *forever*, and I've worn a hat every opening day at Del Mar since 1980.

This picture was taken in our corporate offices in Carlsbad, California, but it's a rare shot of me behind a desk. For most of my career, I was out in the field, interviewing and hiring new counselors for our weight-loss centers and training them to help clients achieve their weight-loss goals. By this time, though, we had competent people to perform those jobs, thus giving me more time to spend at corporate headquarters.

Exercise is an important part of any weight-loss or weight-management program. It doesn't matter *what* you do—or how much—as long as you do *something*. My personal favorite is walking, but I also enjoy riding a bike. This picture was taken on a biking tour of France in 1993 with my daughters and some close friends.

I didn't have a lot of time for vacations during the first few decades of my career, but once Jenny Craig, Inc., was established in the United States and doing well, I finally took the time to see some of the rest of the world with my family. I especially love to travel with my daughters, and this picture, taken in 1987 on one of our trips to Paris, is of Michelle, Susan, and Denise (*left to right*) at the famous Maxim's restaurant. (*Photo credit*: Studio de France et Gérard Delorme.)

Here's a picture of me used in the Jenny Craig, Inc., 2001 annual report. At 71 years old, I'm still active and looking for new challenges. Last year, I took up golf; my 10 grandchildren keep me busy and give me enormous joy; I still travel with my daughters and friends on our fabulous European walking tours; and Sid and I are enjoying our horse racing, as well as still consulting to the company we started 20 years ago. It's been a wonderful life, and I enjoy each new day that comes.

This was one of the highlights of our racing career. Surrounded by family and friends, I'm holding the roses after Candy Ride won the Pacific Classic in August 2003. Julie Krone, the jockey, is standing next to me. (*Photo credit*: Copyright © 2003 by Benoit & Associates.)

Before and after of
Dominick P.

I'm so proud of the accomplishments
of our clients. Dominick P. lost 140
pounds and wrote to us that "it was
one of the best things that ever happened to me…not just because I'm a
thinner person now, but because of
what I've been able to accomplish."

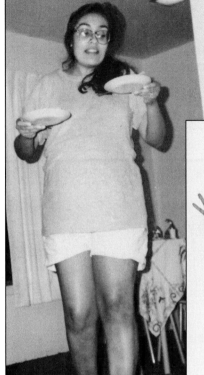

Before and after of
Magdalena B.

Magdalena B. lost 50 pounds
and wrote, "Life is so different
now... I no longer ache when I
get out of bed, and my body
doesn't overheat or tire out
during normal activities...I feel
healthier than ever, and...
getting ready in the morning is
so easy because everything fits."

6

Starting Over:
Back in the United States

"We were both only 52—and ready for a new challenge."

When our two-year noncompete contract was up in early 1985, we returned to the United States. We had kept our home at La Costa in Carlsbad, California, just north of San Diego, because we knew we would be coming back at the end of the two years. Plus, our kids were here: Susan and Steven had worked summers in Australia, but they were still in college in the United States (Steven at USC and Susan at Pepperdine), and Jason was still in high school (and living with his mother). Michelle and her husband and Denise came back with us.

Financially, Sid and I could have retired to live very comfortably on the $10 million our Australian company was sending us each year. But we were both only 52 years old—and we were ready for a new challenge. So we decided to open 12 centers in Los Angeles. That meant leasing an apartment in Century City to be close to our new corporate offices on Santa Monica Boulevard. We

117

opened 12 because to advertise properly and justify the cost of advertising we had to have good coverage of the city.

Getting Started in Los Angeles

Once again, we found ourselves starting out on a new adventure. And getting started in the United States was different from getting started in Australia, because in Australia, there had been no market before we opened Jenny Craig: We had to *create* it. We advertised to explain exactly what we were and what we were going to do.

But in the United States, everyone knew what a weight-loss system was, and NutriSystem had been pounding the airwaves and burning up print in the newspapers, so everyone was familiar with the concept. In our advertising, we called ourselves "the Australian Weight Loss Revolution." John Newcombe, the Australian tennis champion, was our spokesman, but unfortunately most people didn't even know who he was—especially women, and 85 percent of our clientele were women.

Our corporate offices were in Los Angeles, behind the Santa Monica Boulevard Center. There was no need for an intercom system because our offices were so small and close together; we could just shout out at each other. Our office staff consisted of a secretary, a comptroller, an advertising/marketing person, Sid, and me. We continued to operate with that same number of people for the first year and a half.

There are many benefits to keeping the corporate staff small. A small group can better communicate, make quicker decisions, and function better as a team. It also cuts down on the need for a lot of meetings, because every member is in touch with each other on a day-to-day basis, and everyone is up-to-date on changes within the company.

There are many benefits to keeping the corporate staff small. A small group can better communicate, make quicker decisions, and function better as a team.

Later, as our company grew and we added more people to our corporate staff, it became difficult for each group to communicate effectively because the executives in charge of each division became very territorial and protective of their areas of responsibility. Many CEOs of other companies have told me this is a common occurrence in corporate America. It makes me wonder why, if we know keeping it small works better, do we continue to add people just because our financial numbers are increasing rather than assessing the real *need* for more workers? That's one more example of knowing what is best and not doing it.

After returning to the United States, it was great having our La Costa home as our weekend retreat during our temporary move to Century City, and eventually it became our permanent home for about four years.

When we decided to return to the United States, knowing that we would once again have to hire and train new employees, we put together a core staff of people who had worked in the Australian operation. Having those experienced people to help with the training made the classes a lot easier. We also sought out the best doctors who were working or teaching in the field of obesity and researching its effect on the human body.

We sought out the best doctors
who were working or teaching
in the field of obesity and researching
its effect on the human body.

One by one, we assembled our professional consulting staff. Along with other experts in the field of obesity and its health risks, they were:

- Dr. C. Everett Koop, who was the Surgeon General of the United States at that time.
- Dr. Kelly Brownell, professor of psychology at Yale University and professor of epidemiology and public health at the Yale Center for Eating and Weight Disorders. His research focused on eating disorders, obesity, and body weight regulation, as well as issues relating to education and public policy.
- Dr. Frank Greenway, who was the medical director at the Pennington Biomedical Center at Louisiana State University; his area of research was the treatment of obesity with an emphasis on pharmacological and nutriceutical interventions.

New Challenges in a New Market

On the Monday of our grand opening in Los Angeles, there were 11 full-page ads for other weight-loss and fitness companies. Talk about stiff competition: It surrounded us! There was a company called Diet Centers, which had 2,200 locations, and it was plain to see that NutriSystem had a strong presence in the Los Angeles area: It had 1,200 centers nationwide, and both these companies offered food, like we did, that was either canned or freeze-dried.

Moreover, in a sense, anyone who was selling a pill or a shake—that is, any product that was being sold for weight loss—was a competitor. We viewed our competitors as being in two separate categories: one requiring a small investment by the client, the other a large investment by the client. A typical small investment competitor would be one selling shakes, bars, diet books, and other small-item purchases. People who have tried those products are still likely to come into one of our centers. People who have made large investments (over $500) to lose weight and have not been successful are less likely to immediately try something else. In designing our advertising campaigns we tried to appeal to both groups. Testimonial advertising can be very powerful in convincing people that success is achievable.

Our competitors were also advertising aggressively. Disc jockeys on many of the radio stations were plugging NutriSystem because they were successful clients of their program. Back in our days with Body Contour, Inc., we had learned that celebrity endorsements were a great way to demonstrate testimonial proof that the program really works. Back then, we had used television personalities. Because each radio/television personality has a loyal following, his or her testimony is perceived as more believable and credible.

We also advertised all kinds of specials as an added incentive during the time John Newcombe was our spokesman. However, the phone wasn't ringing. People stayed away in droves. So we did a little market research by asking those polled if they knew who John Newcombe was. We got answers like, "Sure, isn't he that basketball player?" We decided that campaign wasn't working, and we ditched it.

So I started doing the TV commercials as our spokesperson, while using Elliott Gould for celebrity recognition (even though he wasn't a client at the time). We were trying to attract men as well, so using both Elliott Gould and me in the commercials appealed to both markets. Later, we also worked with Regis Philbin,

Susan Ruttan (from *L.A. Law*), Cindy Williams (of *Laverne & Shirley* fame), and Jerry Mathers (of *Leave It to Beaver*).

We also tried giveaways with each enrollment: for example, a scale, a pedometer (so people could track how far they were walking), and other gifts that would be helpful to clients in their journey to lose weight. But these giveaways, too, were unsuccessful. We put our thinking caps on and decided that in order to get people's attention, we had to have something different from anyone else. We knew we had by far the best program—one that achieved the safest, best results—but people hadn't discovered us yet. We needed to get our message out there.

> We knew we had by far the best program
> —one that achieved the safest, best results—
> but people hadn't discovered us yet.
> We needed to get our message out there.

It was Sid who came up with the idea of complete frozen meals that could be purchased at the centers. He had had this idea even before we returned to the States. He realized that Americans have a much more sophisticated palate than Australians had at that time. Most of the foods we were selling in the centers we were importing from Australia, and we weren't getting rave reviews. Frozen food is better tasting and offers more variety than food preserved either in cans or in hermetically sealed retort pouches, which don't need refrigeration and can be heated in boiling water. Weight Watchers had frozen dinners, but they were not part of the Weight Watchers *program*, and they could be purchased only in supermarkets. We wanted a one-stop, complete weight-loss program. We immediately began to research the possibility.

We found a company that made food for a French airline, and it was really good-tasting. And we could designate by how many calories you wanted and what the size of the portion would be. We experimented in four or five centers in Los Angeles by offering the foods, packaged in plain white boxes printed with only the name of the food and how many calories it contained. Within two weeks, people from all over Los Angeles were standing in line because they had heard about these centers that had the frozen food. We knew we had a winner, and we went right into production.

Introducing frozen dinners meant we would need freezers in every center, and most centers would need special wiring to accommodate them. Logistically, it seemed like a nightmare. But where there's a strong will, there's always a way. I won't say it was a worry-free exercise. In the beginning, we had freezers go out, and we lost whole truckloads of food. And we experienced other glitches, like the food arriving in the middle of the day when the centers were packed with people and no one was able to help unload the trucks. Eventually, we arranged for the deliveries to be made late at night after the centers were closed. After we introduced the frozen foods, and by word of mouth as well as advertising it became known how delicious and convenient they were, the phones began to ring off the hook. Our U.S. company was on its way!

There were other adjustments to be made in the program. Australian women tend to have larger frames than the average American woman. One example is shoe size. During the time I lived in Australia, I had difficulty finding shoes to fit my size six-and-a-half foot. Most of the merchants carried very few shoes less than size seven-and-a-half because there was little demand for them. There were many styles over size eight. Because of their larger frames, the recommended healthy body weight for an Australian woman was higher than it was for women in the United States. We took that into account when designing the program here.

The computerized schedule for a person's ideal weight was based on insurance actuarial tables. Those tables were designed to determine the ideal weight for each type of frame for a person to expect to be the healthiest and live the longest. When a client came into a center for the first time, simply by feeding (no pun intended) the necessary information (present weight, wrist measurement, height, sex), we could determine what would be a realistic goal weight for that individual. Of course, those schedules were *guidelines* and not meant to be absolute goals. For instance, an athlete with large muscle mass would expect to weigh more than a sedentary person of equal bone structure, because muscle weighs more than fat.

When we returned to the United States we found that it was not easy to locate food companies that were willing to produce small quantities of prepackaged foods for a few centers. We had to convince them there were a lot more centers to come, extrapolating our Australian rate of growth, as we had about 100 centers in Australia at that time. For a while, as I mentioned, we even imported some foods from Australia that were in cans and retort pouches. We didn't offer a lot of choices then, but today we have more than 75 different food selections. Introducing complete frozen dinners allowed us to offer so much more variety in the menus.

Today, Weight Watchers is more of a competitor because they're worldwide, and their brand is in supermarkets so people are seeing it all the time. But interestingly, in spite of all that, when we ask focus groups what comes to mind when you think of weight loss, they say Jenny Craig.

It's important to make our advertising effective enough that people will remember the brand, and that's what we've tried to do. We've tried to build the brand name for that reason, not to promote me as a personality, although it was helpful in the beginning to have someone to talk about the company and draw attention to it. In 1985 the United States was right in the middle of the feminist movement, and I think knowing that a woman was at the helm of the company, working actively, appealed to a lot of women.

We also focused on making sure our sales message appealed to our market. To sell effectively, you need to learn what motivates your customer, and this varies depending on what the product is. In weight loss, usually the primary motivator is appearance—even though there are so many health benefits that are by-products of weight loss, most people are coming in to look better. And once you recognize that, then you know what your dialogue should be. First, you have to create desire, and to do this, you have to find out what's important to the buyer.

I used to ask a standard question in every training class: "If you could give me a one-word definition of sales, what would it be?" And I got all kinds of answers (including *money!*) but to me, that one word is *communication*. If you can't communicate with a person to find out what her needs are, then we had little chance of satisfying that need.

For example, talking about the health benefits of your program to an overweight woman who just wants to look better isn't going to make your program appealing to her. So even though there were many varied benefits to the Jenny Craig program, we always tried to focus on what was important to *each client*.

Expanding the U.S. Market

We continued to expand in the Los Angeles area, and before long had 30 centers. Michelle and Duayne returned to the United States, and they were eager to get to work. We gave them a franchise in Sacramento. They started with three centers, and soon there were seven. Their business was doing well, so they bought a house and started a family. They now have three children: a daughter Sydney (my first grandchild!), born in 1987; Zachary, born in 1988; and Remington, born in 1992. Michelle and Duayne moved from Sacramento to San Francisco and eventually owned 50 plus franchised centers that were all doing well. For them, life was good.

When Denise returned to the United States, she continued her same role in the company, only now she was our international training director. After watching our success in L.A. and seeing the success Michelle and Duayne were achieving, she decided that she, too, wanted a franchise. So we gave her the franchise in Bakersfield, California. Bakersfield's opening was a bonanza. It was the biggest opening of all the California centers up to that date. After a while, we gave Denise the Fresno franchise. That, too, was a success, but not quite the success of Bakersfield.

Later, after Denise married Walter Altholz, a grandson of the founder of Hertz Rent A Car, she and Walter decided to take on Houston, Texas. We gave them the Houston franchise and they packed up and headed south. Walter's formal education was in law, but he had worked for a large sports club chain that gave him some experience in weight management. So both he and Denise were active daily participants in their franchise.

Our expansion primarily happened because people approached us to open franchises. As mentioned, we first opened in Los Angeles, then Chicago, then New Orleans, then Sacramento, when Michelle and her husband moved there. Then, a woman who had worked for Body Contour, Inc., contacted us to become a franchisee in Phoenix. Because she couldn't invest the full amount required, we went in as partners with her and her husband in a franchise; once they were successful, they bought us out.

And we opened in most of the major cities throughout the country this way. For example, a woman who had been in the gym business opened in New York. Most of the time, people approached us. In every city, though, we needed to open enough centers in that city to justify the cost of advertising needed to reach the critical mass.

Going Public

By 1987, the company had 100 company-owned and franchised centers in Australia, eight franchises in New Zealand, six franchises in the United Kingdom, and 39 company-owned and franchised centers already in the United States—only two years after opening in Los Angeles. We were certainly successful by any measure. Yet this achievement wasn't enough for Sid, who had always wanted to be chairman of a publicly traded company. In 1988, Merrill Lynch underwriters contacted us, wanting to take us public. We embarked on a road show, which was grueling: We went to Chicago, New York, Boston, and other eastern cities the first week, and we were scheduled to do the whole West Coast the following week.

Unfortunately, by the time we got to the 11th hour, the climate had changed for the worse on Wall Street. Initial public offerings (IPOs) were not being met with the same unleashed enthusiasm as they had been a few months before. After all, we were in the middle of the Gulf War at that time, plus the economy was suffering from a recession in the aftermath of the stock market crash of 1987. So Steve Koeffler, who headed up the West Coast office of Merrill Lynch, called an emergency meeting in Orange County, California. Merrill Lynch advised us that we would have to go out at considerably less than we had anticipated, because we weren't creating enough interest. We would have to go public at the low end of the range we had been given in the beginning of negotiations.

We decided not to continue with the road show because we would have been leaving too much on the table. We had been told initially that we would go public at $12 to $15 a share (and this was the price range included in the prospectus), but now they were talking in the $10 range, which represented only about $58 million. So we pulled the plug and considered that perhaps later on when times were better we'd make a second attempt. Naturally, we were disappointed, though at the same time we were relieved that we didn't have to continue the road show at that pace: We didn't have a plane at that time, so we had to give a presentation and then dash to the airport with our luggage to make the plane for the next meeting in the next city. We had to hand-carry our luggage on board, because checking it would have caused intolerable delays.

When I think back to our road show with Merrill Lynch, I still find it amusing that most of the people attending the "show and tell" meetings looked like they were about 12 years old. I thought to myself, "Are these the people who make important investment decisions? Where are the grown-ups?" They couldn't seem to grasp the concept that we needed public money to expand, because our past expansion was financed totally with funds generated within the company, and we had no debt. We began to think maybe this public thing was not for us.

We began to think maybe this public thing was not for us.

In 1990, we were contacted to consider a recapitalization, which meant creating debt, something we had never done before. We met with several companies who wanted to handle the transaction and settled on Bear Stearns. Michael Tennenbaum was vice chairman at the time, and he was the one to take us through the whole process.

Michael soon became a good friend in addition to being the leader of that project. I have always admired Michael's genius. I consider him a giant in the financial community, and I would still solicit his advice on any investment. The recap catapulted Sid and me into a whole different financial arena. One hundred ten million dollars were distributed to corporations we personally had control of. We had never had that much money outside the Jenny

STARTING OVER: BACK IN THE UNITED STATES

Craig company before. Of course, for financing the recap we had to give away some of our company in warrants to the investors. We also had to meet certain financial goals in order to maintain our same percentage of ownership. But being able to cash in some of our chips was good financial security.

The company was going from strength to strength, and the financial climate on Wall Street was favorable; so in 1992, we once again decided to take the company public. We felt that the time was right: The company now had 521 centers in the United States alone (in 37 states), 332 of which were company-owned and 189 were franchises, in addition to 118 centers in Australia, New Zealand, Canada, and Mexico. And our annual revenue from the United States centers had grown from $6 million in 1986 to $373 million for the fiscal year ended June 1991.

So once again we set out on a road show, with meetings planned in about 10 cities across the country in less than 10 days; we often did two cities in one day. Like the previous road show in 1988, this schedule of presentations was very tight, but the road show was much easier because by this time we had our own plane; we could arrange our presentations around the time we thought they would take and leave when we wanted, so it wasn't such a frantic pace. Sid and I both participated in the presentations: I answered technical questions about the program, and Sid answered questions about what our marketing plans were and how we viewed ourselves with respect to competition.

This time we had little trouble convincing the 12-year-olds that the public offering was now prudent in order to pay off the debt we had acquired with the recapitalization. This strategy they understood. Go figure!

On the day of the IPO, we were invited to a breakfast with the top honchos at the New York Stock Exchange. When we arrived at one of the boardrooms, I saw that I was the only woman in a room with about 10 blue suits. I could tell from the polite and solicitous conversation that they were unaccustomed to having female guests.

When we first sat down, Sid turned to me and asked if I would tell a story he had heard me tell before. At first I refused, thinking it would be in bad taste, but, after his urging, I succumbed.

The story goes like this: A female flight attendant learned that Gloria Steinem was taking her flight. After Gloria's arrival, she knelt down next to Gloria's seat and whispered, "Oh, Ms. Steinem, I'm so excited to meet you. I know how you've championed women's rights. I couldn't wait to tell you that our air-traffic controller is a woman." Gloria seemed pleased. The attendant then said, "Ms. Steinem, our *co-pilot* is also a woman," and Gloria applauded and seemed even more excited. The attendant then said, "Ms. Steinem, I saved the best for last: Our *pilot* is a woman." Upon hearing this information, Gloria was exuberant and exclaimed, "Oh, I'm so impressed—I think I'll go to the cockpit to congratulate them." The attendant then said, "Oh, Ms. Steinem, we don't call it *that* anymore." The men all seemed to love the joke, and I think they felt a little more at ease after that. I guess that story made me seem more like one of the boys.

I wish that I could describe the emotions I was feeling as I walked onto the floor of the New York Stock Exchange. All around me there were traders with boxes of Jenny Craig products stacked on their counters. Some were yelling that they had lost weight on the program. Others were just giving us a warm welcome. Then I saw it: My name began to appear in lights and circle the floor in ticker-tape fashion high above us. I was speechless. There aren't adjectives to adequately describe the exhilaration of that moment. Whenever I question our decision to go public, I think back to that time and I realize that no matter what, I wouldn't trade that experience for anything.

The IPO was a success; in fact, it was even oversubscribed. We came out at $22 a share, which represented a valuation of $500 million—almost 10 times the expected valuation of our company during the 1988 aborted IPO. As we stood there on the floor of the

New York Stock Exchange, we watched the stock price jump three points. Because we personally still owned 75 percent of the stock, we calculated that Sid and I had just made $80 million in less than 30 minutes (albeit only on paper). Perhaps the dot-com success stories have distorted our perspective, but back then that was a very exciting gain in the first hour of trading.

> We watched the stock price jump three points. Because we personally still owned 75 percent of the stock, we calculated that Sid and I had just made $80 million in less than 30 minutes.

After we left the Exchange, we went walking along Fifth Avenue and Sid said, "We should buy something to commemorate this auspicious day." I have a black belt in shopping, so I didn't need convincing. The only thing Sid saw that he wanted was a $500 watch, and I still find it hard to believe, but I didn't see one thing I wanted and didn't already have. Whenever Sid wears that watch (one of a collection of more than 50), we talk about that day. I don't have an object to remind me, but I don't think I will ever forget that day.

Running a Public Company: Making Changes

So, now Jenny Craig, Inc., was a publicly traded company. Probably everything you've heard about being public is true. Yes, it is exciting watching the stock reports in the morning. Yes, it is a way of establishing the dollar value of a company. Yes, it is a way to retrieve some or all of one's initial investment. Yes, when things are going well, it is a way to let the world know without having to boast.

But there are not-so-obvious negatives, too. You are a target for anyone or any group to take shots at. There are endless papers that must be filed each year at significant costs to the company in dollars and manpower. There are outside board members who must be compensated and whose approval you must elicit when any change takes place. You tend to think in terms of the financial quarter results rather than the long-term payoff. A shareholder owning 10 shares can call our CFO, Jim Mallen, to question our wisdom on some decision or action the company has taken. He or she may have no understanding of the company or its business, yet that person still expects a detailed explanation.

Also, you tend to reject any venture that takes time to build momentum if it's going to negatively impact the next quarter. For example, when we first introduced frozen dinners, we really felt that would give us something different and separate us from the competition because no one else had them. But there was no guarantee that was going to happen, and we had to make a sizable investment: to buy freezers, to have all the centers rewired, to have all the frozen dinners made in large quantities. Had we been public at that time, it would have required a lot of serious thought to see how it would impact the quarter—which illustrates how worrying about the bottom line sometimes makes one leery of introducing new things or making decisions that could dramatically affect the bottom line. So you have to either promote a change aggressively or abandon it immediately if it's not successful. These are just a few of the pros and cons of going public.

Another challenge we faced as a result of being public had to do with the franchisees. For instance, if we wanted to run a special promotion or advertisement without any additional cost to the franchisees, or give them any kind of perk during slow times, we were afraid of being accused of self-dealing, because our children were franchisees. That was unfortunate because we have always tried to develop a good and profitable relationship with all franchisees. We have always considered each franchisee an extended family member and an integral part of our company. We wanted every one of them to be successful, so any help or relief we could give them we gave willingly.

We eventually decided to buy back the franchises our children owned. We felt it was a good financial move for the company and it would release us from the fear of self-dealing accusations. We bought back Northern California, Houston, Riverside, Fresno, and Tampa, Florida. Over the years, we have bought back other franchises as well, all for different reasons.

Now that Duayne and Michelle were no longer franchisees, they began to look around for another business in another industry, because they didn't want to compete with us in the same industry. I mentioned to Duayne that I thought there was a real void in the party supply industry. I have given *lots* of parties, and each time I did, I could never find all the things I wanted to create a theme party, whether it was a Halloween party, a Valentine's party, or a St. Patrick's Day party.

I told Duayne I thought there was a tremendous market for that, and that if I were going into a new business, that's what I would be looking for. So he started doing research on the Internet, and he attended a franchise exhibition in Las Vegas. He found a business back East that had five stores, called Party City, which was doing quite well selling many inexpensive products to create a theme party.

Duayne visited the owners of Party City to get more information and to find out more about how he should go about getting into the business. Surprisingly, they said they were considering a private placement so that they could expand the company, and they asked if Duayne would consider investing with them. He discussed it with us, and he set up an appointment for Sid and me to meet with the founders/owners. When we met, we were impressed with both of the founders and with their presentation. We learned that Steve, the president, had vast experience not only in the party business but also in other businesses that inventoried thousands of products. We decided to invest in the company, along with Duayne.

Duayne wanted a franchise in Chicago, his hometown and a city with great potential in that business. Our decision to invest proved to be a good one. Our initial investment of approximately $2 million was at one time worth about $30 million, once the company went public. We still own most of our Party City stock, and although the stock is currently trading for considerably less, we remain optimistic that in the future that company will bring us even greater profits.

7

Health Troubles
and Legal Problems

*"Surely there's something or someone out there that has
the answer."*

In 1995, I had a serious personal setback in the form of an accident. I was watching TV while sitting on a couch with no headrest. I fell asleep and my head fell forward with my chin resting on my chest. A loud noise from the TV awakened me with such a start that my head shot up, snapping my lower jaw up over my upper jaw. I had to pry my teeth apart. To say I was frightened is putting it mildly.

I began to lisp as a result of trying to keep my lower front teeth from hitting my upper teeth. I went to my dentist to see if he could help me. He said he had never seen anything like my condition, and he referred me to a temporal mandibular joint (TMJ) specialist. That was the beginning of many consultations with many specialists over the next two years before I finally found some relief.

The TMJ specialist told me my jaw had dislocated. Normally, there's a gel-like substance that cushions the condyle (the bony prominence at the end of a bone where it forms a joint with another bone, in this case between the mandible and the skull), and this substance allows your jaw to articulate—that is, to open and close. In my case, however, because it had been a week or more since the accident that caused my injury, so that gel-like substance had been replaced by scar tissue, nothing short of surgery on the joint would work.

The specialist did not recommend surgery, because then-current results were not good. This specialist lectured all over the world, and he had done many experiments, so I had good reason to go along with his advice. In addition, there was so little information at the time on injuries of that type, because little research on it had been done. Now there's more information on this problem.

The TMJ specialist suggested I try wearing a dental appliance to alleviate the problem. My jaw wasn't *simply dislocated*, as in permanently dislocated; it was (and still is) *chronically dislocating* when I speak. So he made a form for my teeth, and we tried all different kinds of appliances: First I wore one for my upper teeth, then I tried one for my lower teeth. Finally, he made an appliance that fit under my tongue and covered my molars with no visual appearance on the front teeth.

All these appliances were awkward to wear and to handle, plus they had a further disadvantage in that I had to remove them whenever I ate out—and Sid and I ate out a lot! But more important than the awkwardness, discomfort, impracticality, and embarrassment was the fact that none of the appliances solved my problem: They were only a Band-Aid.

My TMJ doctor had also recommended physical therapy on my face, so I tried that next. Unfortunately, I quickly became disillusioned with this approach as well. At first, I had a therapist who was very knowledgeable and very good at what he did, but then one day when I went in, this very young woman who looked about 12 years old said, "I'm going to be doing your treatment today."

When I asked for my regular therapist, she dismissed my request by saying, "I'm a colleague," and she started working on me. I let her get started, but my initial misgivings about her got even worse because she kept asking me questions as though she didn't even know what she was supposed to do. So I said, that's it; no more of this.

Searching for Traditional Medical Treatments

I decided to go to Los Angeles, to the UCLA medical facility's head and neck specialists. I had X rays taken of my jaw; MRIs to determine if I had suffered a stroke; and various neurological tests. But all these tests revealed nothing: The MRIs showed I hadn't suffered a stroke, so nothing had affected my brain; and the neurological tests revealed that there was no nerve damage. The medical specialists there said everything was ideal, that I was in perfect health, to which I replied, "That's wonderful! But why can't I speak better?"

I thought if I could diagnose what the problem was, then we would know how to cure it. But nobody could come up with a diagnosis. But I kept trying to find out, doing research on the Internet, and reading health letters from the Mayo Clinic and Harvard. Somewhere in my search, I found out about a New York dental specialist who was described as a specialist of speech disorders, and I made an appointment. After just a brief examination, he diagnosed my problem as dystonia, which he said might have evolved from a trauma to my jaw.

That specialist referred me to Dr. Mitchell F. Brin, who was head of neurological disorders at New York's Mount Sinai School of Medicine. Dr. Brin confirmed that I had focal dystonia. He had spearheaded research in dystonia, which is irregular movement of any area of the body—that is, involuntary spasms and muscle contractions that induce abnormal movements and postures. *Focal dys-*

tonia affects a single part of the body, such as the eyes, neck, arm, or vocal cords—for example, eye twitches or a tremor in the hand. (*Multifocal dystonias* affect several noncontiguous parts of the body, such as the eyes, hands, and vocal cords; there are also other types of dystonias.)

Dr. Brin said he was getting good results by injecting Botox into muscles. I hadn't even heard of Botox—this was only 1996, before Botox was widely known—and Dr. Brin certainly wasn't recommending it for cosmetic reasons. The *Merck Manual*, in fact, today cites Botox as the treatment of choice for patients with focal dystonias. Dr. Brin thought that by paralyzing the muscles that I was using to speak would force me to use other muscles. My accident had started out as a trauma, and then evolved into dystonia. I was compensating for not being able to speak by trying to protect my teeth, which were knocking together. When my jaw dislocated, my lower teeth came forward; now they would hit my upper teeth, which would send a shock up the front of my face on the side of my nose. So to prevent that from happening, I had put my tongue in the way, which made me develop a whole different set of speech patterns.

Dr. Brin's theory was that if he could immobilize the whole set of muscles I was using, then it would make me speak normally. So we started the treatment the next day: He gave me 12 Botox injections in my face, and these were the most painful injections that I have ever endured—believe me, worse than what I experienced while giving birth to my daughters. He injected Botox into the masseter muscles located outside the cheeks. He then injected the pterygoid muscles located both inside and outside the mouth. He also injected other small muscles that aid in opening and closing the jaw as well as for articulation. There were tears rolling down my face; it was so very painful.

The treatment helped briefly—a couple of weeks, maybe, but

that was all. (Similarly, Botox treatments that people get today last only a few months.) Therefore, Dr. Brin was going to have to do this series of 12 injections every three months or so. When I realized this, I decided not to pursue the treatment. I felt that I would rather talk the way I was talking; the cure was worse than the problem.

Nevertheless, I greatly appreciated the fact that Dr. Brin was able to accurately diagnose my problem, and I think he's a wonderful, caring doctor. And I still correspond with him occasionally, to this day. He took such an interest in my whole case, and he was just as kind as he could be.

Exploring Alternative Medicine Treatments

Unfortunately, I still didn't have any relief from the occasional pain and discomfort in my jaw, not to mention the difficulty I continued to have simply in speaking. I had tried the traditional medicine route, and when I didn't get satisfaction, I thought, well, let's see what else is available; let's look to alternative treatments.

Someone had told me about a place called the Upledger Institute in Palm Beach Gardens, Florida, so I researched it on the Internet. I learned that it was founded in 1985 by Dr. John E. Upledger, an osteopathic physician, surgeon, researcher, and teacher. From 1975 to 1983, he had been a clinical researcher and professor of biomechanics at Michigan State University, and during those years, he had supervised a team of anatomists, physiologists, biophysicists, and bioengineers in experiments testing the existence and influence of the craniosacral system, which provides the physical environment in which the brain and spinal cord develop and function. The craniosacral system comprises the membranes and cerebrospinal fluid that surround and protect the brain and spinal cord.

Dr. Upledger had pioneered craniosacral therapy (CST), which is a hands-on method of evaluating and enhancing the function of the craniosacral system. According to the Institute's web site, CST is effective for a wide range of medical problems associated with pain and dysfunction, including migraine headaches, chronic neck and back pain, motor-coordination impairments, TMJ, and many more serious problems—from autism to spinal cord injuries.

The therapists at the Upledger Institute help people with all kinds of neurological disorders and injuries. Essentially, they do this special type of physical therapy using their hands. Dr. Upledger discovered that the body has different rhythms, and he feels that many neurological problems that people have are related to these rhythms, which can be controlled. It made sense to me, and even though the Institute was expensive, I decided to go; I decided to try it. My daughter Michelle had a home on Jupiter Island, Florida (though she was living in Chicago at the time), so I stayed there. And I started the treatment: The therapists pressed different parts of my head—particularly in and around my mouth—in order to control the median rhythm and to determine what area was producing the malfunction. So in addition to treatment, it was also a diagnostic technique.

I was there for a week, and every day they worked on me for about eight hours. They were sincere in their efforts, hoping that the treatments would do the trick. Obviously, I couldn't stay in Florida forever, so I returned to California. When I came back home, I was rested, but my speech was no different. Dr. Upledger had given me the name of a cranial therapist in San Diego, so I went to her three times a week for a while, but again, there was no real change in my condition. What the therapists had done didn't help me. It wasn't their fault; there's simply not a lot anyone could do for my condition, at least not with a therapy-based treatment.

The next treatment I received was again nontraditional. My Pilates instructor suggested I try acupuncture. He told me he had seen wonderful results, and he gave me the name of his acupuncturist, who was an M.D. who had studied in Japan. I also heard of another doctor who was achieving very good results through acupuncture, and I chose her because she was closer to my home. Dr. Ni tried many different techniques, some using high-frequency electric stimuli that were generated by placing attachments to the acupuncture needles that had been inserted into the soft tissue of my face. Sadly, that didn't change things for the better, either.

So there I was, still without any improvement. The next person I heard about was a doctor in Boston who was achieving all kinds of amazing results using "healing hands." He wasn't a physician, but he had a Ph.D., and he had been profiled on *60 Minutes*. So I flew to Boston and told him my story. He put his hands on my jaw, and his hands got so hot—simply through energy—and I reasoned, "This must be doing some good." But in spite of the hour-long session, I still had no resolution of the problem.

He wanted me to continue, to stay there for four or five weeks, but I couldn't. After the treatment, nothing about my condition had changed or improved, so I thought this was going to be just like the Upledger experience. Before I went to him, I probably would have thought the guy was a quack, but I was grasping at straws: I would have tried *anything* to see if it would work. Each time I tried something new, I thought, "This approach is going to work; this is going to do it." But it didn't. Still, I really tried to maintain a positive attitude.

I would have tried *anything*
to see if it would work. . . .
I really tried to maintain a positive attitude.

I even tried psychotherapy at some point during this time. I went to the Scripps Clinic in La Jolla, California, and a doctor there referred me to a psychotherapist, because I'm sure they thought this thing was all in my head. So I went to see him. He was a psychologist, and from my medical records, he was aware that I had physiological damage to my jaw. But he felt that the accident had traumatized my *brain*, and he wanted to try to erase that. His treatment consisted of trying to erase the *memory* of the incident. His theory was if I could erase the accident, then my mind wouldn't know it happened, and my body would compensate.

He recorded each of our sessions and gave me the tape to take home, asking that I play it several times a day. Each session was a different approach to accomplishing the same objective. Because the sessions lasted one hour, the tapes were also one hour long, so playing them several times a day required quite an investment of time. His sessions were directed to first get me to relax, thus relaxing all the muscles that were affected. His approach was to have me erase the whole incident, sending the message to my brain that nothing had ever happened to my jaw at all. He asked that I envision myself speaking the way I normally did before the incident. His theory was that if it never happened, then my brain would figure a way to return my jaw to the position for normal articulation. It was a kind of hypnosis, really, to induce me to forget that it ever happened to begin with.

To be frank, in at least one way this approach helped me more than anything, but it didn't cure me. It helped me simply because it relaxed me. As with any trauma, what happens is that all the affected muscles become very traumatized, as though in a spasm. After I listened to his tapes, I *felt* like I was talking better because my muscles were more relaxed.

Over a span of two years, I took many tests and was treated with various methods by 17 different doctors all over the country. Without exception, they all said in one way or another, "I've never

142

seen a similar case. I don't think I know how to help you." I had tried physical therapy, acupuncture, cranial therapy, Botox, psychotherapy, healing hands, as well as many dental appliances—all without much success. Yet I continued to search for a solution, because my speech was becoming more and more impaired. Sid thought I should just accept that I had a speech impediment and learn to live with it instead of raising false hopes for recovery. But I refused to give up. I still thought, "Surely there's something or someone out there that has the answer."

> Sid thought I should just accept that I had a speech impediment and learn to live with it. . . . But I refused to give up.

However, by then I had concluded that my problem was purely mechanical and nothing short of a mechanical adjustment would fix the problem. I knew that articulation of the jaw depends on so many parts operating with such synchronization that even just one of them not firing at just the right time can create abnormal speech.

A Surgical Approach

I continued to search the Internet, and I read current medical journals, still looking for some treatment that might help me. One day, I happened to be watching a local TV station and saw a reconstructive surgeon explaining the fantastic results he had achieved with cleft palates and cleft-lipped children in his photos. His work was being done pro bono through a program he had founded called Fresh Start. I thought there might be a chance he could help me.

His name was Dr. Dennis Nigro, and I contacted him immediately. This was in May 1998—three years after the original accident. His office was nearby in Encinitas, California. As he examined me, he explained that he thought my facial muscles were stripped because I was using my tongue to support my jaw. In doing so, I was severely affecting my speech. At times, it was difficult to understand what I was saying. He said he could perform surgery that would reattach the damaged muscles, but he couldn't guarantee that my speech would greatly improve since the neuro-pathways were destroyed. Because it had been so long since the incident, I had developed different patterns of speech.

Dr. Nigro believed that if my jaw had been wired *immediately* after the incident, I would not have developed the altered speech patterns, because my jaw would have gone back in the joint, and the scar tissues would have formed around the condyle. Then when the wires would have been taken off later, I would have been able to speak normally. Unfortunately, none of the doctors or specialists I had seen had even suggested this would have solved my problems. They just didn't know what to do. At any rate it would have been too late.

I was willing to take the chance that one day I could return to a normal way of speaking. We scheduled the surgery for June 10, 1998. When I came out from under the anesthesia, Dr. Nigro explained that he had never seen muscles so shredded. He said he could see my teeth through the muscles. He had to reattach the muscles with self-dissolving screws that he had designed.

When I looked in the mirror after surgery, I was horrified. I looked like an alien from another planet. I thought, "What have I done?" As soon as the swelling and the bruising cleared—about a week after the surgery—I began speech therapy to retrain the muscles involved.

Dr. Nigro recommended speech therapist Marlowe Fischer. She turned out to be a delightful trainer. She enthusiastically worked with me every day for almost a year, working on my speech patterns. She would have me speak certain words with certain combinations of vowel sounds—somewhat like Eliza Dolittle in the movie *My Fair Lady*. I still have volumes of exercises that she gave me: Every time she came to my house, she gave me a new sheet of exercises.

She started with single words; then she introduced phrases, then sentences. For example, at first I tried to speak simple words like *cab, cage, calf, call, calm, came, can, cap, car*, and so forth—usually 50 words with a related sound (in this case, obviously the hard "c"). Then, once I had "graduated" from one-syllable words, she asked me to speak phrases and full sentences, again to work on a particular sound.

Each session, we would first go through the exercises, then Marlowe would say, "Now let's just sit and talk." She wanted to see if I was applying anything I had learned during the exercises in my regular speech. Then she would tell me what she wanted me to concentrate on, and she gave me homework to practice.

She came to my home an hour each day, and after she left I continued to practice for another four or five hours. Perhaps I overdid it, but patience has never been one of my strong points. I wanted to improve as soon as possible, and I was willing to do whatever it took.

> Patience has never been
> one of my strong points.
> I wanted to improve as soon as possible,
> and I was willing to do whatever it took.

I did ask Marlowe how long I was going to have to do the therapy. I had seen people who had gone through strokes and then speech therapy, and after a year they were speaking almost normally again. But Marlowe said my case was actually harder than with stroke victims, because I had to *unlearn* how to speak. In contrast, a stroke victim only has to *learn* to speak, the same way a child does. But in my case, I had to unlearn the speech patterns I had developed and then learn to do it right, which was doubly hard. After a year, I cut my sessions with Marlowe to three times a week, though I continued to practice every day. By 2001, three years after my surgery, she was coming to my home only once a week, and the practice went on. By 2002, I stopped the therapy sessions.

After all the treatments I've been through, I've come to believe that my whole problem is a mechanical, physiological problem. I could have improved the movement in my jaw still further with additional surgery, but this would have required the surgeon going into my ear to have the mandibular joint put back in place permanently. I had gone to a doctor earlier to see about that, and he said, "I'll be happy to do your surgery, but if you do it, you could end up with a lot of pain and no correction." To which I replied, "Enough said." That was too big a risk for me; thankfully, I have no pain now, and that is good enough for me.

I don't think I will ever return to my old way of speaking, but I am thankful that at least I can communicate with people. I would have done *anything* to prevent or avoid what happened to me. Unfortunately I didn't have that choice. When I look around and see all the suffering in the world, I'm thankful for what I have. Yes, my accident did impact my life dramatically, and there were times I thought, "Why me?" And there have been times when I prayed to wake up from this bad dream, times when I felt discouraged because I couldn't see noticeable results from my efforts. It was at those times that I would remind myself of the things I should be celebrating. I am very healthy, I'm able to exercise daily, I can still work, I have people who love me, and I have a lot of fun. I have a good attitude, and attitude has a lot to do with recovery and good health.

My Injury Affected My Business, Too

After my freak accident, because of my speech impediment I was no longer able to do commercials for the company. We had different celebrities, but nobody really replaced me. In 1999, we used my daughter Denise as a "new Jenneration" at Jenny Craig, and we returned to using celebrity spokespeople, which had always worked for us in the past.

In a way, it wasn't the worst news for me that I could no longer be the spokesperson, because I got back a little more privacy. There were times while I was doing the commercials when it was difficult to shop for groceries: People would check my grocery cart to see what products I bought. People would ask me, "Do you recommend that brand?" or "How do you feel about that kind of bread or milk?" or about anything I bought or had in my cart. I always responded, "Well, this is just what I like; I don't really have any particular brand recommendations."

And when Sid and I went out to restaurants, people from across the room would often deliberately go out of their way to walk past our table to see what I was eating for dinner. The owner of one of my favorite restaurants, Red Trackton's, told me even *he* was often asked by other customers what I usually liked to order for dinner. He said he always jokingly answered, "Broiled mockingbird tongues."

I've also had people interrupt my dinner asking for diet tips or an autograph. I never mind hearing about weight-loss success stories; I welcome them because they always make me feel good and proud of what I do. But some people just want to know your innermost secrets or pretend they are your best friend to others around them.

One time, I even heard a story broadcast on a local radio station that said, "Jenny Craig was in Von's grocery store today, and the manager said that Jenny had bought Weight Watchers food." When I heard this, I called the station and told the station manager that simply wasn't true. And when our marketing vice president called the manager of Von's, he said he didn't know what we were talking about: He said, "I don't know Jenny Craig. I don't even know what she looks like. That wasn't me saying that; I never made that call." It was just a prank: Someone had called the radio station and pretended to be the manager.

Those are the drawbacks to celebrity, but there are many benefits, too. For instance, it has always been easy for Sid and me to get a table in the busiest of restaurants. And I've had the opportunity to dine with many famous film stars and with five U.S. Presidents, as well as many other celebrities.

I met Paul Newman, for example, years ago, and he later wrote an endorsement for one of my books, *Cutting Through the Fat*. (He wrote, "*The Jenny Craig Cookbook* is a dining delight . . . a memorable experience between the covers.") I met Paul initially at a charity function that Sid and I attended in 1993. It happened that Paul and I both worked with the same publicist, Warren Cowan, a very well-known public relations guy (of Rogers and Cowan fame) who represented many famous Hollywood stars. Warren had also done a lot of publicity for the Jenny Craig company and in the process had become a good friend of ours. Paul told me all about the Hole in the Wall Gang Camp, in Ashford, Connecticut: He had provided the seed money for this organization when he first started selling his Newman's Own salad dressings. Sid and I have since made donations to the camp, which is for children with cancer or blood diseases.

After that function, on one of my visits to New York to promote my book, Warren called Paul and told him I was coming. Paul invited me to lunch at a quaint place he had frequented over the years. We had a very nice lunch, but the highlight of the day came later, when we dropped Paul off at his Manhattan apartment. As he said goodbye, he leaned over and kissed my cheek, and I thought, "My God . . . this is Paul Newman!" Before that day, just the thought of being kissed by the man would have made me faint.

Another fascinating event was meeting and dining with Sidney Poitier. Sid and I were in the Bahamas with Merv Griffin, whom we had met earlier. Merv had been on the Jenny Craig program and had lost a considerable amount of weight. He had appeared on a talk show and mentioned that fact, and as always, he was terrific. He later did a commercial for us. He has become a good friend, as we share many of the same interests, including tennis, horseracing, and games of chance. Merv had invited us to his resort on Paradise Island for a tennis tournament. While there, we visited Merv's Casino, which is part of his vast empire. Sidney Poitier was also there.

I told Sidney how I had admired him all these years, and he was very gracious. He said, "Well, I've really admired you, too." He was my dinner partner, and he was undoubtedly the most delightful man I have ever met. It was such a pleasure to be there, and the stories he told were so charming. He joked that for years he wouldn't have gone back down there (to the Bahamas, where he grew up on Cat Island) because he "probably owed everybody down there money." I'm sure he was joking.

I've also enjoyed meeting Sally Field and Liz Taylor at a dinner party, when Liz was married to Larry Fortensky. And Sid and I met Harry Belafonte in Monte Carlo in 1993. We had sponsored a tennis tournament for the Princess Grace Foundation, and Harry Belafonte was performing there; he was also staying at the same hotel. We went to his performance that night and were seated right by the stage. I told him I had a longtime friend, Joanne, who had lusted after Harry when she was younger, and I kidded him about this. And he is a very sexy guy. So he posed for a picture with me to give to my friend, and as the flash went off, he said, "Joanne, lust away!"

I met Sean Connery as well that night: He and his wife also were attending Harry's performance in Monte Carlo. As we were leaving to go to the casino, Sean's wife said to me, "Put everything you've got on number four." We played roulette, and I said, "I'm going to do what she said," and I put it on number four, and it hit! I won a lot of chips, but I hadn't bet a lot of money. Still, it was fun to win, because it was so odd that she had suggested my winning number.

I'm also proud that I've met five U.S. Presidents: Gerald Ford, Ronald Reagan, George H.W. Bush, Bill Clinton, and George W. Bush. I met George H.W. Bush at Rupert Murdoch's home in Beverly Hills, where Sid and I had attended a campaign fund-raising party for him. Later, we met George W. at a private dinner; he came to our table, and I told him the only Bush I hadn't met was his mother. And George W. told me, "Then you missed the best one." I loved that he said that.

I met Ronald and Nancy Reagan at a tennis tournament that Nancy had sponsored, which I played in. One of my partners was Pancho Segura, who had been one of the best tennis players of his time; I also played with the legendary "Lone Wolf" Pancho Gonzalez there. But Segura and I made it to the finals, so afterward I had an opportunity to talk to Nancy and Ronald Reagan.

I don't mean to drop names; I only want to point out that these were experiences that I found interesting and delightful because I had the opportunity to talk to these famous people personally, and I got to ask the questions of them, rather than the other way around. Those were some of the perks of celebrity. Thankfully, I still enjoy friendships with some of those people, even though I'm no longer in the spotlight, and I cherish the fun times we've spent together.

Although my disappearance from our commercials gave me back some degree of privacy, it also changed the direction of our advertising. I was no longer the spokesperson for the company. We continued to use testimonials from our clients, which had always worked in the past. I believe people are more convinced that something will work for them if they have visual proof it has worked for others facing the same challenges. In our early days, I was helpful in putting a face to the brand. Now I was no longer necessary as a spokesperson because we had worked hard to build a brand name and not necessarily one with a recognizable spokesperson—in much the same way Betty Crocker and Sara Lee are brand names of women we don't know.

I believe people are more convinced
that something will work for them
if they have visual proof it has worked
for others facing the same challenges.

In our early days in Australia, we were faced with the reality that we didn't have any clients yet who had achieved success on the program, so we couldn't advertise with testimonials. That was what we knew had always worked, throughout our entire career in the industry.

Having no testimonials when we first started the company meant I had to do the commercials to tell the viewers what Jenny Craig was all about until such time that our clients had achieved enough success to advertise. I can candidly tell you, I wasn't good at that then. Whenever I look back at those early commercials, I cringe from embarrassment. Perhaps I never did become good as a spokesperson, but I can say I got a hell of a lot better.

The change in me was really learning to relax and talk to the camera in the same sincere way I had always talked to people and not from a memorized script. Often the director just filmed me talking, with no structured script. I talked about things I genuinely believe in, things I knew were necessary for success in weight management. I think those were the best commercials I did. However, commercials now are presented in time segments of 30 to 60 seconds, so most directors require a script with concise timing so that very little editing is necessary. That was the format we used in most later commercials; still, they were always *my* words.

Legal Problems

Life was good! But, it was not free of challenges. In addition to my jaw trouble, Jenny Craig, Inc., faced some legal problems. The first arose during one of my visits to Florida for the grand opening of our Miami centers. I was scheduled to appear on a local talk show. When the interview began, the host blindsided me with his first question: "What's all this about NutriSystem causing gallbladder problems?"

Well, I didn't have a clue what he was talking about, though I found out later that there had been accusations that the NutriSystem program caused gallstones. I told him I couldn't comment on that accusation or NutriSystem's problems. I didn't know what else to say, so I reiterated that there was proven evidence that weight loss from a supervised, sensible, credible program of healthy eating, combined with an active lifestyle, was beneficial to one's health, especially for people who have potential for heart disease, diabetes, and hypertension. I try to always be prepared before I show up for an interview or a speech, but I had not yet heard of those accusations (which, by the way, were later proven to be unjustified). That was the beginning of a long list of challenges for the company.

There were actually a *series* of lawsuits naming NutriSystem as responsible for a number of gallbladder problems. One such suit was a class action involving a number of people. Although Jenny Craig, Inc., was not named in those suits, I believe they inspired some political opportunists to jump on the bandwagon and attack the weight-loss industry as a whole. A Congressional panel was created to determine what the guidelines should be. That panel was headed by Ron Wyden, a Congressman from the state of Oregon (he's now a Senator).

As participants and leaders in the industry, we, along with Weight Watchers, were invited to attend. Sid decided that I should not attend personally as I would be fodder for the media. Because I was the only one whose name was on the door, and the most recognizable figure, their focus would have been on me.

We selected Ellen Destray, one of our vice presidents, as the one who should represent the company. It was televised and we watched the whole proceedings. Ellen did an outstanding job, but it was easy to see there was a strong political agenda in progress. The panel disagreed with our method of advertising with testimonials. For example, they said we couldn't advertise how much weight a client lost over a certain number. They told us we couldn't say that someone lost more than 50 pounds because the panel claimed such losses were atypical—which was so ridiculous, considering that so many other companies had people claiming their satisfaction with various products in *their* ads.

> ## We couldn't say that someone lost more than 50 pounds because the panel claimed such losses were atypical.

After the lawsuits were filed, the Federal Trade Commission (FTC) asked for a cease-and-desist agreement that all players in the industry would have to sign. We were already practicing many of the guidelines the FTC was proposing, but other guidelines were ridiculous and would have made it difficult to run our company. So we fought back. We felt our rights under the Constitution were being usurped.

We enlisted proper legal advice and proceeded to challenge some of the directives the FTC was demanding.

I understand the FTC's job is to protect consumers, but we had never made any kind of ridiculous claims that some of the pill companies did, so we didn't feel that we needed to make any big adjustment in our advertising as far as *truth in advertising* was concerned. Nevertheless, this panel was requiring us to make changes to our verbiage so that it would satisfy them. But we also had to find something we could live with from an advertising point of view.

Another example of what we saw as the FTC's unreasonable requirements was that if we advertised a price (like any type of special), we had to also include the price of food. We had always said in print, as well as in broadcast media, that the food costs are extra, but that didn't seem to satisfy them. Because food cost varies depending on what foods are chosen, we felt that saying that the food costs were extra and not included in the price of whatever special we were running at the time was self-explanatory. Not even the credulous could possibly think that when we advertised "20 lbs. for $20" that that price included all the food one would eat to lose 20 pounds! So we had to negotiate what was acceptable verbiage that we could live with and still not in any way misrepresent what a client was paying for and receiving.

I objected to the FTC's initial requirements because I felt that, on the one hand, the government was complaining about the lack of healthcare and the cost to the average American for a prolonged illness, and on the other hand, it was trying to destroy an industry that offered its participants a healthy lifestyle conducive to preventing disease. There was enough credible research and information that was made public for everyone to know that obesity is a leading cause of life-threatening diseases, such as heart trouble, stroke, some cancers, as well as diabetes.

Furthermore, obesity among children has doubled in the past decade, and it is close to overtaking smoking as the leading cause of sickness and death.

The biggest challenge Sid and I faced in our business was getting through the NutriSystem lawsuits. In addition, we were the victims of a frivolous lawsuit. After the NutriSystem suit gained so much publicity, lawyers in every state decided to jump on the bandwagon. We were sued, and the plaintiffs didn't even bother to remove NutriSystem's name in the papers they filed: Several times throughout the lawsuit, NutriSystem's name was there instead of ours! I won't go into the whole ordeal from start to finish, but suffice it to say that we and our insurance company settled out of court for $12 million. We only had to pay $2 million.

The biggest challenge Sid and I faced in our business was getting through the NutriSystem lawsuits.

Now, here's the rub: The settlement was supposed to benefit the clients who had been on the program, but all our clients got were coupons toward the future purchase of food and products. The lawyers got *$10 million* from the settlement. I consider that legal extortion. This lawsuit affected us not only financially, but emotionally. It's very draining; you get so angry thinking that the insurance company covered $10 million of the $12 million, and the attorneys got the $10 million.

We had so many of our clients return the coupons, saying they were outraged and didn't feel they were entitled to the credit, because they had received good value for their investment. Besides,

where is the rationalization of offering coupons for future purchases on a program that the plaintiffs were trying to prove to be
unhealthy? Am I missing something?!

I am truly embarrassed for the legitimate lawyers who conduct
their business in an ethical and moral way. Our lead attorney, Marvin Sears, is that kind of lawyer. He has counseled us for over 20
years and I greatly admire his honesty and dedication to doing
what's right. Of course, as with all industries, everyone in it
shouldn't be painted with the same brush. But, there are some un-
professional, unethical lawyers in that industry and we should all
do what we can to keep them from ripping off the public. Tort re-
form is long overdue!

The entire episode also saddened me. We Americans are taught
that if we work hard and conduct ourselves in an ethical and moral
way, we can achieve success in business, and doing so can enable us
to realize the American dream of ownership. What they fail to
teach us is that once we become successful, we become a target to
destroy. We become the enemy to the bureaucrats in Washington.
That's known as "cutting down the tall poppies." Shouldn't a company that offers help to people struggling with their obesity, trying
to improve their health, be *nurtured* by government agencies instead
of being *attacked*? Do they have so little to do constructively that
they search for targets to attack?

Big business employs people who pay taxes. Big business itself
pays taxes that allow those same agencies to exist. Why do those
same government agencies look for reasons to destroy their source
of support? I have difficulty grasping the rationalization of that
concept. Do they really think that consumers are so dumb that
they need someone to audit their choices before it's safe to make
them? Do they really believe that we, as consumers, are incapable
of making intelligent decisions on our own? Sure, there are companies in our industry that make ridiculous claims and promises, and

those should be made to comply with ethical standards set by the industry. But, please, don't throw the baby out with the bathwater. There are those kinds of companies in all industries. Please, don't paint everyone in the industry with the same paintbrush.

Since our first day, Jenny Craig, Inc., has conducted our business in the most ethical and moral way with sincere efforts to offer value in a program designed by professionals to assist clients in weight management. Our track record shows results that speak for themselves. We receive hundreds of testimonials each year. Here are just a few excerpts from some of the wonderful letters we receive every day from clients who are grateful that we've been able to help them change their lives:

> I'll never forget the moment I decided to change my life around. It was May 2000, and I was cleaning out my closet . . . before I started a new job. I discovered my clothes ranged from a few size 8s to my then-current size 14s that were getting tight on me. . . . Right then and there, I called the Jenny Craig Centre in my town. . . . Before I knew it, I was a size 10, then a size 8, then a size 6 where I felt so comfortable. . . . Life is so different now. My cholesterol is lower, I no longer ache when I get out of bed, and my body doesn't overheat or tire out during normal activities. I feel healthier than ever, and . . . getting ready in the morning is so easy because everything fits!
>
> —Magdalena B., lost 50 pounds
>
> I am writing to earnestly thank you for my rebirth, reawakening, and new life. . . . I lost 31 pounds on

your program and have kept it off for four years. I know it sounds like a cliché, but I can't believe how it has changed my life.

Like many, weight gain just kind of crept up on me. I was not in the habit of exercising regularly, nor did I have healthy eating habits. . . . But it didn't occur to me that I could possibly gain weight or be overweight. . . . And it didn't get through to me when the local hospital, after going in for a routine medical test, sent me some literature on the health hazards of obesity. Surely, I assumed, it was an error. Not me!

I was profoundly shocked, when attending a health fair at my children's school, that I weighed close to 200 pounds. First came depression, then resolve . . . to be a healthier person for my family. . . . After losing weight and gaining confidence, . . . I feel I can do anything I choose. I feel like a teenager asking myself what I want to do when I grow up, and all these exciting options are open to me. Thanks again for helping me to find this new me that was buried inside.

—Susan V., lost 31 pounds

I can still remember that Saturday evening in July when my sister Vickie and I were planning to meet some friends for a surprise birthday party. The one thing that went through my mind was, "No matter how lovely the outfit you wear, the clothes aren't going to hide the fact that you are larger than you have ever been." At 267 pounds, I was ready to do something about my weight.

I called Jenny Craig and enrolled. . . . I had originally planned to lose 80 pounds, but once I reached that and felt and looked so good, I decided to continue. I've lost 114 pounds and have never felt better in my life. . . . I've discovered a new self-awareness, have more confidence, and can trust myself to make healthy decisions. Keeping a positive attitude has helped me become a living illustration that what you can imagine yourself to be, you can become.

—Veronica, lost 114 pounds

After I gave birth to my third child, the weight would just not come off. My weight had climbed to 180 pounds . . . after weighing only 130 pounds before I got pregnant. Over the next year, I managed to lose 20 pounds on my own, but I couldn't seem to go any further to shed the remaining 25. On September 29, 1995, I joined Jenny Craig.

I know now that was the most positive step I could have taken. . . . Today, I feel wonderful! I am a very devoted mother, but I had often told my husband that the birth of our children had inadvertently caused me to stop taking care of myself. . . . Now, people who see me 20 years after I graduated from high school think I look exactly the same. I'm also much more active with my children, and am glad I can model healthy eating and exercise behaviors for them.

—Stephanie G., lost 25 pounds

Those letters and others like them are what inspired me to continue working hard at helping people take control of their lives by making positive changes to their lifestyles. On many occasions, there were tears on my face as I opened my mail and read those heartwarming letters. Reading each life-altering success story gave me the feeling that I was doing something important.

8

The Challenge
of Succession Planning

*"I have always believed we should have a woman in
charge of all field operations."*

Before my jaw troubles and the legal nightmares we endured in the
1990s, Sid and I also faced problems as we tried to find successors
to lead Jenny Craig, Inc., into the next generation of management.
We decided to bring in an outside president and chief operating officer, knowing that one day we would begin to step back a little
from the day-to-day running of the business.

Sid hired an executive search firm whose president elected to
take on the search himself. As he learned about our company and
interviewed applicants, the more our recruiter thought *he* was the
most qualified to fill the job. We don't know if it was conscious
or otherwise, and we will never know whether his desire to take
the position distorted his evaluation of all the applicants. I only
know that he seemed to be better qualified than all the applicants
he presented to us. So, we appointed him to be our new president and COO, while I relinquished those titles and became
vice-chair of the board.

161

I won't go into all that was wrong with our decision, but, suffice it to say it didn't work out. Being the head of a company whose job is to acquire and keep franchisees happy is not the same as running a company that requires good marketing and field training in sales as well as constant monitoring of the financials. The prior job does little to prepare one for the other. He didn't remain in that position very long.

Culture Clash

Realizing that we had made a mistake, Sid began to look for a replacement. We decided to hire a former NutriSystem executive whose expertise was in marketing. Immediately upon joining the company, he started making changes that resembled the NutriSystem's culture, which didn't match Jenny Craig, Inc.'s culture at all: He was trying to convert Jenny Craig, Inc., into another NutriSystem, which just didn't fly. We felt that NutriSystem treated its employees as though their talents were unimportant. In other words, they felt as though *anyone* could do the job.

At Jenny Craig, Inc., our culture was different; we felt our employees should be on the balance sheet, because they were so integral to the success of our business, and we always treated them that way. We have placed great value on each of our employees. My philosophy has always been that any business is simply four walls and people. No matter how great your product or service is, without good people, you have nothing.

Moreover, at NutriSystem, all the supervisors and all the people in the home office were men. And we felt they were male chauvinists, which was obviously a mismatch with our company—85 percent of the clients and 95 percent of the staff are women. I had felt that way since 1982, when Harold Katz bought Body Contour, Inc., and the Gloria Marshall Figure Salons. If you recall, he offended the audience at our sales convention in Las Vegas by telling locker-room jokes and then later made a list of all the women earning more than $50,000 a year because he felt that no woman should be earning that much money. I had hoped, of course, that this manager would be different, but Sid and I were finding out that wasn't the case. We just didn't realize how pervasive that culture was at NutriSystem.

In addition, our new president also started making capricious employee cuts without even knowing how important each employee's contribution was. He didn't bother to ask, "What's this employee's record? How important is she?" Instead, he just said, "We'll get rid of this one and that one," as though he were going down a list. The result of these cuts was that people in the corporate office were beginning to think, "I could be next!" Because he had no regard for the value of each employee's contribution, his style of management was directly counter to that of Jenny Craig, Inc.

After three months, we realized our new president wasn't the right person.

As it turned out, though, we didn't have to terminate him. One Monday morning when we arrived at the office, we found his office was dark. One of our employees said, "I think he's gone." We looked around his office, and sure enough, all his belongings were gone. We never heard from him again: He never called us; he never wrote us a letter of resignation—nothing. We had never seen or heard of anything like that, especially since this was a senior executive, not some junior or entry-level employee! We had sent out a press release to the stockholders announcing his having been hired and then he had disappeared. It was so bizarre. But at least he was gone.

Focusing on the Wrong Things

You're probably thinking by now, "Give it up as a bad idea!" Well, I guess we're slow learners, because we didn't abandon the idea of

163

trying to find a qualified person to serve as our president and chief operating officer. We began to think that one of our outside board members would be right for the job. He knew a lot about our company, and he had held positions as president and senior executive at other large corporations. We presented the idea to the board, and they approved hiring him as president and CEO. We all looked forward to his administration.

The new president thought that because we had grown so fast, our focus had been on designing the program and developing people to work in the field, with little emphasis on our home office environment and functioning. He felt it was necessary to add some structure to the corporate team. That sounded right to us initially, and we respected his previous experience in corporate management. However, the reorganization of our home office had not been of primary importance to us.

We have always viewed the people at the front line who daily service and support the clients as the ones who contribute the most to our overall success. They are the people who make the business work. To every client who comes to a Jenny Craig center, her counselor really *is* Jenny Craig to her. And whether that client is successful or unsuccessful in meeting her weight-loss goal depends greatly on her interaction with the person she's dealing with day to day.

> We have always viewed
> the people at the front line
> who daily service and support the clients
> as the ones who contribute the most
> to our overall success

So, while we expected our new president to follow through with his ideas and plans for creating structure in the home office, we were surprised to see him spend most of his time doing that to the exclusion of what Sid and I thought was paramount to achieving success in the centers. We saw him as a micromanager who required endless reports and focused on the details rather than looking at the big picture.

We have always viewed the corporate staff as a backup to what goes on in the field. Our job at the home office was to create effective advertising and marketing campaigns, organize and distribute training material, provide assistance when needed, distribute food and products in a timely fashion, and support the field personnel in any way we could.

The new president's management style was very different from the way Sid and I ran the business. In the end, the culture clash between our different approaches was too much for us to live with. I'm sure our differences were apparent and frustrating to him as well. To make a long story short, we decided to part company, at a sizable financial cost. Under his contract, we had to pay him more than $3.5 million.*

Radical Program Changes—But Not Improvements

If you're thinking, "Well, now they've learned their lesson," I must disappoint you once more. Yes, believe it or not, when we learned that another former executive from NutriSystem was available, we decided to try again with a new president from the outside. We had met him when we were in Philadelphia working for Harold Katz and NutriSystem, and we liked him. We also knew he was the only person we met during the time we worked for NutriSystem who really understood the *psychology* as well as the *physiology*

---

* Jenny Craig, Inc., annual report, 1995, p.31.

of weight management. He had a history of weight challenges. So once again we had a new president/COO.

While he was with us, he made some decisions that have had costly ramifications. For example, he introduced a program of meal replacements in the form of bars and soups, called "Jenny Craig on the Go," for women who were too busy to take the time to eat a proper meal. In order to get this program off the ground, we had to buy *a lot* of inventory, and we had to sign a contract with the vendor to produce enough for us to restock regularly.

When we introduced this program, many new clients thought, "Well, I'll try this first." Unfortunately, these clients weren't successful in meeting their weight-loss goals, because even though we told clients that this was a meal *replacement*, they often ate it *in addition* to their regular meals. So, obviously the program didn't work. But we still had to honor our commitments to the vendor, plus we still had all the inventory we had taken on. That was a huge and costly mistake.

We were learning succession planning the hard way. What happens when you have people come in from outside the company is that they seldom say, "What can I do to improve this the way it is?" or "What can I contribute to this company?" Instead, they say, "What can I *change*?" Everybody is looking for some kind of glory; everybody wants to be a hero. They want to come in and change the whole operation, and then it's going to be a super-success. But Sid and I knew from experience over the years that no matter what comes and goes, successful weight management always depends on the fundamental fact that one simply has to exercise more and eat less. And that's it.

And a client has to have a program she can live with. If you're going to do something short-term, you have to expect short-term results. So with those on-the-go things and short-term Band-Aids, if you will, that's all you're going to get: short-term results, instead of the permanent solution of a healthy lifestyle. And that's the thing that so many people have trouble with, because everyone seems to be looking for a quick fix.

The one good thing this last new president did was to cure us of the fantasy of finding a good leader from outside the company. We said, "You know what? That's it." We had tried every resource that we thought could possibly be effective, and none of them worked, so we just gave up.

Even though we abandoned the idea of finding someone from outside the company, we still had to face the reality that one day in the not too distant future, through either health challenges or normal aging, we would have to let go of the reins at Jenny Craig, Inc. It would be foolish of us to wait with no future planning until a crisis that required us to do that presented itself. So we began to think of other options.

Promoting a President from Within

Of course, as time went by and all this was happening, Patti Larchet was getting stronger and stronger. She had been running our Australian operation since 1993 when we had promoted her to managing director, which is the equivalent of a COO. We realized she was the ideal candidate to be president of the U.S. operation, and in 2000, we asked her to come back to the States and take over.

Patti had been with the company since our initial expansion into Chicago, her hometown, in 1985. She joined us shortly after receiving her nutrition degree from the University of Illinois at Urbana–Champaign. She truly worked her way up through the ranks: She started as a counselor in the Chicago area in 1985, but she quickly became a center director, then a regional manager. In 1988, she was named National Sales Trainer, with responsibility for all centers in the eastern United States as well as some foreign operations.

167

In 1990, she moved to Australia as director of operations, with the long-term plan that she would return to the United States. She proved to be invaluable to the success of our Australian operation. She got great publicity for us; she lined up terrific Australian celebrities—including a famous soccer player and a soap opera star. As mentioned, we promoted her to managing director as soon as we realized that she was considering remaining in Australia. The main reason she was planning to stay there was that she was in love and pledged to marry John Larchet, who was residing in Australia and working for an advertising agency there. (They did marry, and John has since developed a company that exports fine Australian wine.)

Patti increased revenues in Australia by nearly 90 percent from 1993 to 1999, and she improved profits as well. In 1994, Australia had an operating loss, but by 1995 it was profitable, and by 1999 it had an operating income of nearly $9 million (U.S.). She increased the client base; she increased the average time clients were on the program; she improved service; she improved everything about the Australian operation.

In fact, by 2000, Australia was doing better, per center, than the U.S. operation was. And even though Australia represented only 10 percent of the number of centers we had, they were more profitable than the U.S. centers were. Patti was a hero.

> Australia was doing better, per center,
> than the U.S. operation . . . even though
> Australia represented only 10 percent
> of the number of centers.

Then we learned she was pregnant. We hoped she would choose to continue to work as well as be a mother. She is a true professional and very dedicated to her work, so after her son Benjamin was born, she returned to us and continued to break all records of production in Australia. In addition to mastering the business, Patti is a typical client: She gained 65 pounds during her pregnancy, and she had been a yo-yo dieter all her life. But she incorporated the Jenny Craig program into her own life and learned to manage her weight.

Her husband was spending more and more time in the United States because Americans were buying more of the fine Australian wines that he exports. His contacts and commitments were increasing, and the growth of his business required that he spend more time here in the States. So things worked out well when we asked Patti to return to the United States. After deliberation and consultation with John, she accepted.

Putting Patti in charge of operations was the single best move we had made in years. I have always believed that we should have a woman in charge of all field operations, because 98 percent of our employees in the field are women and 85 percent of our clientele are women. That's *not* a sexist remark. It makes sense that women relate best to other women.

A woman understands what other women want and feel. A woman knows from experience the challenges other women face when they are trying to make positive lifestyle changes. It follows that a woman should be calling the shots. It wasn't long after her arrival back in the United States that we promoted Patti to both president and COO. For the first time since I had stepped down as president, we had a woman in charge of all field operations, program design, and marketing, and not just *any* woman, but one who had grown up in the business and knew every level of operation. Hallelujah!

A woman knows from experience
the challenges other women face
when they are trying to make
positive lifestyle changes.

Patti quickly proved to be the right choice. She began a vigorous retraining program, targeting new and innovative changes in the program. She hired a female vice president of marketing—the first of many senior-level women. (I've always been proud of the fact that overall 95 percent of our employees are female, including the top levels of the company.) After Patti's return, for the next couple of years, this was the first time the company had a woman president and a COO, a woman head of operations and training (we had always had a woman in charge of training), *and* a woman vice president of marketing—in other words, in the three key revenue-generating positions.

Patti also hired a new advertising agency—a boutique agency, instead of a large agency. Weight management is an unusual category to understand in terms of marketing, because the agency really needs to understand the mind-set of our target clients. Patti wanted to go back to a boutique agency because she'd had great success with them in the past. And she wanted to work with an ad agency that had some women on the creative side. She found Johnson and Ukropenia, a small boutique agency in Orange County that's run by Caroline Johnson and Joyce Ukropenia. After Patti came on board, we hired them, and we've been with them ever since because they are just terrific. It was the first time we'd worked with a woman-owned agency, but they just clicked with the brand. They all immediately went on the program, and they still have our business, three years later.

Patti's changes proved to be good strategic moves. The number of calls from potential customers began to increase. The number of enrollments increased. People were staying on the program longer because we had made it easier for them to do so.

We were now offering more choices and more flexibility, keeping in mind that people need a certain amount of structure when making changes in their lifestyles. It's also important to make sure the menus are nutritionally sound. With the new Ultimate Choice program, clients could feel more in control while knowing they were safely losing weight and enjoying the whole process.

The impact Patti made began to be reflected in the bottom line. Each quarterly report showed positive results of her efforts. We were thrilled that for the first time we had a president that had come up through the ranks, understanding the process at every level.

You might wonder why we hadn't brought her back to the United States sooner. The answer is simply that she wouldn't have been ready earlier. It wasn't until she had successfully run the 100 centers in Australia that she was ready to take on an additional 550 centers.

I've always believed that advancing in business is very much like lifting weights. You don't start out lifting 100 pounds. You start with 20 pounds. And you gradually build up, thus preparing your muscles to handle the extra load as you increase the amount of weight. Success happens when preparation and opportunity cross. You must prepare so that when the opportunity comes, you can be qualified to take on the task. Patti proved that she was now ready to face the challenge of running 650 centers located in four countries, some of them on different continents.

> Advancing in business
> is very much like lifting weights.
> You don't start out lifting 100 pounds.
> You start with 20 pounds.

In addition to bringing Patti back to the United States, there were other management changes. After five years of cold Chicago winters, my daughter Michelle missed sunny California. She had fulfilled her promise to her husband, Duayne, to spend five years in

Chicago to establish his Party City franchise, but in 1999 they decided to move back.

Once Duayne realized that Party City was not a business that could be run successfully with absentee management, he elected to sell his franchise to the parent company when they moved back to California. They settled in Rancho Santa Fe. I can not overstate how happy I was to learn that for the first time ever I would have three of my grandchildren within a couple of miles of my home. Before this, all of our grandchildren lived so far away from us that plane travel was necessary in order to spend time with them, meaning our time together was less frequent than I would have liked it to be. Now seven of them are so close, I can visit them anytime I want to.

We offered Duayne the position of chief administrative officer at Jenny Craig, Inc., headquarters, and he accepted. We knew he could contribute a lot in that position because of his experience of owning and running more than 50 Jenny Craig centers in San Francisco, Sacramento, and throughout Northern California. It has worked out well for us both.

Promoting Patti and watching the success that came as a result helped to make me realize that it was time for younger people to take control of the company. Sid was almost 70, and I wasn't far behind him, so it was time for us to move on and relinquish control.

Stepping Down from Day-to-Day Operations

During all these changes, I remained in the background. After our first outside president left, Sid asked me to give each new president full authority, because people should answer to only one leader. I realized he was right. If for no other reason than out of habit, people would have come to me for advice or information, which could conflict with the new president. I have always subscribed to the philosophy that you can serve only *one* master. I re-linquished my title, little by little. During the years when we were changing presidents, I transferred my titles of president and COO and took on several other titles in the process. First, I went from president to COO; then when we appointed Patti as COO, I be-came vice chairman.

I had started cutting down my hours before my accident, in 1995. And with the hiring of each new president, I spent less and less time at the office. It wasn't as though one day I left; it was grad-ual. Still, it was difficult at first for me to leave the office behind. Af-ter all, I had gone to work every day of my life for 48 years, taking only three months off for the birth of each of my daughters. I felt like a fish out of water.

But, I realized, too, that I now had some free time to do the things I had never had time for before. I had time to develop closer friendships. My women friends became my pals with whom I could sit around and just talk girl talk. I had time to plan trips to places I had always longed to visit, but was too busy to do so before. In 1994, I started taking my three daughters and two very dear friends on a two-week trip every year—usually a walking trip (arranged by Butterfield and Robinson), and we've since gone to Spain, the Tus-cany region of Italy, Austria, and the Burgundy region of France.

Walking is the best exercise for women (especially women who are still in their child-bearing years). Jogging is not as good, be-cause it's harder on the joints. Plus, walking is more enjoyable for me because I can appreciate the environment so much more: To me, it's very calming, even though I walk fast. (In fact, Sid won't walk with me because he says I set too fast a pace!)

My daughters and friends and I also went on a biking trip through France, mostly through Provence. That was quite a trip! Those all-female trips are highlights in my life. We've stayed at quaint villas and country inns, laughed a lot, eaten the finest foods, laughed a lot, and met wonderful people—all enjoyed while adding years to our lives by walking an average of 12 to 15 miles a day. Oh, and did I mention we've laughed a lot? Each trip has been special in its own way.

I enjoyed having the time to travel and to see more of the world. But best of all, spending less time at the office enabled me to enjoy the company of my grandchildren for longer hours and more frequent visits.

I was beginning to settle into my new lifestyle and enjoying its many benefits. That extra free time came in handy later when I had to devote so much time to recovery after my accident, and especially after the surgery, in 1998. I could spend that time in treatment without feeling guilty, thinking I should be at the office, which would have created additional stress.

I believe that unfortunate incident made both Sid and me realize that we were not the invincible couple we had always believed ourselves to be. All during our years together, neither of us had been sick. Neither of us had missed a day at the office due to illness. I had never before experienced the feeling of helplessness. I always felt in control, able to conquer anything that came along.

It's funny how a freak incident can change your perspective on things. For the past 42 years, my routine has been to exercise daily and eat healthfully; not smoke; drink alcohol moderately; challenge my mind with new material because I vowed to learn something new every day; and in general, lead an active and interesting lifestyle. I did and continue to do all those things because I enjoy them and also because I feel they are preventative measures to keep me well. I had never considered that some physical disadvantage would be the reason for my retirement or partial retirement from the business.

As I told Larry King during my third interview on his show after he asked me how I coped with the trauma, "I have good health, my beautiful family are all healthy, I have a loving husband, success in business. I have all the material things I need.

Why should I dwell on the one negative in my life?" We can't afford to squander one day with self-pity—life is too short—we must enjoy each and every day in order to avoid regrets of lost happiness or adventures missed.

I have good health, . . .
a loving husband,
success in business. . . .
Why should I dwell on
the one negative in my life?

9

Moving On and Looking Ahead

"I devoted most of my adult life to helping people make positive changes."

I was delighted that we had solved our management problems, and the company was happy with the success our new president, Patti Larchet, had brought to Jenny Craig, Inc. But our stock price wasn't improving—no matter *what* we did. There might have been a blip for a month or two, but we couldn't achieve a sustained growth. This wasn't fair to the shareholders—or to us. We realized we were never going to bring the stock price back to what it once was. We felt that probably all of the bad publicity surrounding the NutriSystem lawsuit—which, again, we weren't even named in!— had adversely affected how people viewed our stock, and many investors probably just decided to move on. So we thought someone new coming in might be able to generate new enthusiasm.

Our company was certainly undervalued: It was trading at only $1.50 a share, but we had about $50 million in the bank, and we carried no debt. I think it was trading less than what our cash was, which is ridiculous, but we didn't know what to do to bring the stock price up. No matter how successful the company was, no matter how the increased profits showed a positive trend, our stock

176

price didn't reflect it. We alone couldn't seem to improve the value of our company. We felt we needed new partners with outside resources who could take the company to what it could be.

Weight Watchers, a company that just two years before had been losing money, had just gone public, and it had been valued at more than $3 billion. We believed we had a better concept, showing better long-term results with an easier and more convenient method of weight management. Our brand was top-of-mind recall when weight loss was mentioned.

According to independent market research, we were considered to be the class act in our industry. So why didn't the public place the same high value on our company? Our stock eventually reached an all-time low of slightly over $1.00. That changed only slightly—even with our announcement to put the company in play! I guess I will never understand the mentality of Wall Street, which in itself is a good enough reason for us not to be there.

Perhaps we should have remained a private company and never entered the public arena. In any case, our prospects for going back to being a private company looked promising.

> ## Perhaps we should have remained a private company and never entered the public arena.

Searching for a New Partner

In August 2000, we contacted Steve Koeffler and Associates, an investment banking firm, to explore the possibility of acquiring an international partner who could expand our horizons or, if necessary, buy part or all of the company in order to increase its value to our stockholders. We didn't know which direction to go in, whether to go with an international partner who could expand the brand into new foreign countries, or whether we should find someone to buy us outright.

During the search process, we interviewed about 15 companies who were all interested in forming some kind of an alliance with our company. Most of them were financial groups, but one group was from one of the largest companies in the fitness industry.

Some of these companies were interested in a merger of one type or another. Others were interested in an outright purchase of the company. It was important to us that there be a good fit and that the new partners/buyers have the ability to add value to what we already had. It was interesting—and flattering—to us how reverent most were about the brand. We knew that some of their comments were probably solicitous; still, it made us proud to know that outsiders recognized our efforts to make the program credible in its design and efficacy and that we also provided a nurturing workplace for employees.

It was evident that every one of those interviewed really wanted some involvement with Jenny Craig, the brand. After a lot of questions, much discussion and deliberation, along with recommendations by our outside board members, we decided on a partnership with a group headed by ACI Capital Company and DB Capital Partners, the private equity arm of Deutsche Bank.

I think one of the reasons we felt they were the right partners is that Kent Kreh, the former CEO of Weight Watchers, was going to be involved. He certainly knew what foreign markets would be receptive and ready for our type of program. Kent was one of the few people of the groups we interviewed who had years of experience in our industry.

We wanted someone who had a similar business, experience in a service industry, experience in food distribution, or at least *something* in common with our company, because we knew that someone coming in who knew nothing about any of those things would find it a monumental task of understanding how our business works successfully. And if the new people didn't understand the psychology of weight management—if they had never had a weight problem or couldn't understand and appreciate the challenges facing overweight people—that would be even worse. So we were delighted to hear that Kent would be involved because he had been instrumental in turning around Weight Watchers. And we welcomed his objective eye to point the way to our company's full potential worldwide. And today, Kent is chairman of the board of Jenny Craig, Inc.

The group offered $5.30 a share ($115 million), which represented a 68 percent premium to the stockholders. Actually, if one considers that before our announcement to put the company in play, although the stock was still grossly undervalued at just a bit more than $1.00, the selling price represents more than a 400 percent premium.

Life after Jenny Craig, Inc.

Once the papers were signed, I began to think of how my life would change. I had devoted most of my adult life to the work of helping people make the positive changes that improve their health, enhance their looks, elevate their self-image and self-concept, and possibly add years to their lives. I have always felt good about that. My work has always been fulfilling, both in terms of what it accomplished and the feeling of achievement that came with the company's success. As to the change in my routine, the worst was over for me.

It happened when I first stepped down as president, transferring that responsibility to an outsider. That was really the first cut in the umbilical cord. That meant that I would have to remain in the background. It would have been difficult for another president to

179

call the shots while I still remained active. Intellectually I knew that, but emotionally it was difficult. When it first happened, it took all the discipline I could muster to relinquish control.

It would have been difficult for another president to call the shots while I still remained active.

As the saying goes, "time heals all wounds." As others took over my responsibilities and I began spending less and less time at the office, while filling my time with other things I had long wanted to do, each day got easier. In reality, what I should be feeling now that the company was sold, I felt with the appointment of our first president, as well as with each successive president. In a way, I am grateful that the transition was more gradual for me than the suddenness that occurs with the loss of a job or a business. And I will continue to read all my mail from clients who have achieved success on the program. I love hearing about the positive changes that have taken place in their lives. Those letters are day-brighteners, and I have always looked forward to reading them.

Sid's is a different story. He has been there at the office working as the CEO since day one. He will have to come to terms with the reality that someone else is in charge. He will experience the sudden demise of the greater part of his life. I don't mean to generalize, but I think it's harder for men. They don't easily find a replacement for their work. For Sid, going to an office every day is so much a part of who he is. Some friends expected it to be harder for me because my name is on the door and the company is linked so strongly to my identity. But, as I pointed out, mine was a more gradual withdrawal. Also, believing that the new partners will make

180

the company bigger and better, as well as one we can continue to be proud of, made it easier for me.

I know it will be more difficult for Sid to adjust. Unfortunately he doesn't like to travel, and outside of business, tennis and race-horses are his only interests. He will have to expand his interests to keep busy, and I have faith that he will. Besides, we will still maintain 17 percent of the company. It will be fun watching it grow to what we know it can be. We will both continue to con-tribute the benefits of our many years of experience by working as consultants. Sid meets and talks regularly with the CEO and chair-man of the board, giving him the benefit of his marketing experi-ence. I do public relations for the company, meeting with supervisors, hosting awards ceremonies, and appearing on the *To-day* show and in other media. Working as consultants only means that our hours will be different and fewer, so who cares that there are no titles for that function?

A New Business: Horse Racing

Fortunately, our life hasn't been just the weight-loss business. Both Sid and I have always loved horse racing. Sid has owned thorough-breds since the mid-1970s. Years before, after my brother Bobby re-tired, he began training racehorses. That encouraged me to get more involved in the sport. So as horse-racing enthusiasts, we both envisioned future involvement in the *business* of racing horses. After returning to the United States, Sid and I purchased several claiming horses. We won quite a few races, especially considering how few horses we had.

Things began to get more exciting after Sid purchased a mare named Paseana that had raced in Argentina. Ron McAnally, our trainer, called Sid to tell him the horse was for sale. The first race she ran in this country, she ran second. From then on, she dominated the racetrack. She won her following seven races, including five Grade one stakes. She won the Apple Blossom at Oaklawn, the Spinster at Keeneland, and the 1992 Breeders' Cup Distaff at Gulfstream Park by a whopping four lengths. She was voted champion Older Mare in both 1992 and 1993 and received the prestigious Eclipse Award in both those years. Her record was 29 starts (all in stakes), 14 wins (10 Grade ones), 10 seconds, and one third. She was top money earner, with winnings of more than $3 million. If we weren't hooked before, Paseana made us avid enthusiasts of the great sport of horse racing.

Watching her race was like watching poetry in motion. She is now retired and so far has given birth to only one filly. We named her Paseana's Girl. We also named our farm and training center Rancho Paseana. We have had many more racehorses with decent records, but Paseana has a special place in our hearts. She was awarded the highest honor a racehorse can receive: She was inducted into the Racing Hall of Fame in 2001. No horse ever deserved it more.

In 1992, Sid turned 60 years old. I wanted to do something special for him to celebrate that significant milestone, so in 1991 I began looking to buy a racehorse for him. I wanted a two-year-old who would be eligible for the Kentucky Derby in May 1992. I not only wanted one that would be eligible, but a true contender.

At the eleventh hour, after reviewing a lot of prospects, I still hadn't found the horse I was looking for. Then Ron McAnally called me about a horse in Europe, but it was very expensive. His name was Dr. Devious. Ron said he was willing to go over to check it out as a possibility. From Europe, he called me to say that the horse was a magnificent specimen and his X rays proved him to be very sound. That was the good news. The bad news was they wanted $2.5 million for him. After much deliberation, I said, "Go for it!"

It was getting close to Sid's birthday and the horse hadn't gone through quarantine yet. So, Ron put together a video that I could present to Sid at the weekend celebration I had secretly planned for him. I had planned a weekend in the desert at the La Quinta Resort with 120 close friends invited. It took place one week before his birthday of March 22. That same weekend, there was a champion tennis tournament being played. So I asked Merv Griffin to write a note to us inviting us to the tournament as his guests, giving us a reason to go there.

Merv was so kind to offer his home for the first night's celebration. His home in the desert is truly magnificent. When we arrived at Merv's, most of Sid's college buddies along with our dear friends were there to greet him. He was surprised, of course, but I think Eva Gabor gave the secret away early when she greeted him at the door and said, "Happy Birthday." He knew then that something was up. As he stepped from the foyer into the room, everyone yelled, "Surprise!" as he realized what was happening. It was a glorious weekend, with parties on Friday and Saturday nights as well as fun activities during the day. The celebration culminated at breakfast on Sunday.

At the Saturday night party, Jack Jones entertained us. Some of Sid's buddies got up to say what his friendship meant to them. The late Senator Ken Maddy and Coach Jerry Tarkanian were among the speakers. They had both been roommates with Sid at Fresno State. Then I got up to present Sid with my special gift. By this time, Sid had done a lot of celebrating and I don't think he quite understood when I showed the video and said, "Sid, this is a video of Dr. Devious. He is my gift to you and he will run in the Kentucky Derby." The room exploded with applause as many people there knew the significance of having a horse for such a prestigious race. Sid just smiled. We all partied until very late into the evening.

The next morning, as Sid's head began to clear, he asked me how much I had paid for the horse. I responded that it wasn't in good taste to ask the price of a gift. After all, I didn't ask him how much he paid for jewelry and other gifts he had given me. He said,

"You don't understand. It will be in the papers tomorrow. I need to know." Finally, I told him, "Two and a half million dollars." He laughed and said, "No, really, what did it cost?" I repeated my answer. I thought he was going to have a stroke. We had never before paid more than $350,000 for a horse, so it was a shock to him, to say the least. He later learned that people were calling me a dumb broad for getting conned into paying so much for that horse. But I remained optimistic that he would win the Kentucky Derby.

On Kentucky Derby day, though, I was nervous. The favorite in the race was Arazzi, owned by Allen Paulson. There was so much hype as Arazzi paraded around the grounds. He was truly a celebrity horse. I thought, "Dr. Devious has his work cut out if he is to beat Arazzi." Sadly, he didn't win the race. Our new horse finished seventh, but he did beat Arazzi, who finished behind him.

After the Kentucky Derby, Sid decided that because Dr. Devious was a European bred horse, we should ship him back to England to run in the Epsom Derby, the oldest and arguably the most prestigious race in the world. We entered Dr. Devious and arranged for him to remain in training with an English trainer, Peter Chappel-Hyam. John Reid, an Irish rider, would ride him in the Derby. With our trainer, Ron McAnally (who had helped me find the horse) and his wife Debbie, we set out for London. That was an exciting trip.

On Derby day, there was a lot of press coverage about Dr. Devious having been a birthday present to Sid. I'll never forget the stretch run. The announcer was saying, "And here comes the birthday present." As usual, English spectators remained calm and silent. But not us: We were cheering him on as loudly as our lungs would allow. As the horses neared the finish line with Dr. Devious in front by four lengths, the announcer yelled, "Jenny bought the present for the Kentucky Derby . . . and he's winning the *real* Derby!" I'm sure every Brit feels that theirs is truly the *only* Derby.

After the race, I was interviewed and asked how I felt about the win. I replied, "I just went from being a dumb broad to a genius in two minutes." We were invited up to the Queen's Box where we met the Queen and the Queen Mum, as well as other Royals. They all were very cordial as they congratulated us on the win. The Queen told us that in all the years she had horses, she had never won the Derby. That convinced us how truly lucky we were.

Dr. Devious also won the Irish Championship for us. He also ran in the Arc de Triumph as well as the Breeders' Cup and the Japan Cup. He didn't win those races, but he earned $1.5 million while we had him. He was purchased from Sid by a Japanese racing stable for $6 million. So he turned out to be one of my better investments. By the end of 1992, we had won a total of 15 graded stakes races (10 of them Grade ones) with only three good horses in our stable. We thought, "This is an easy game." How wrong we were. We have never had another year like that again, or even close to it! We have had lots of fun with horse racing and we can tell many stories of what could have been. And the excitement continues: In August 2003, our horse Candy Ride won the $980,000 Pacific Classic race, in Del Mar, California. The jockey who was supposed to ride him was Gary Stevens, who was the jockey on Seabiscuit, but Gary got injured in the Arlington Million race a few weeks prior—the similarities with the Seabiscuit story and his jockey, Red Pollard, are so spooky. So we had to get another jockey, and we chose Julie Krone, the only female jockey in the Hall of Fame. Candy Ride broke the legendary Secretariat's Belmont track record for a mile and a quarter. Candy Ride established himself as a candidate for the "Horse of the Year" and the Eclipse Award for champion older horses. Sid said it was probably the most exciting moment of his racing career—because it doesn't get any better than winning in your own backyard!

What I've Learned about Success in Business

Throughout the years, I have received many letters with questions on what I think it takes to be successful in business. My answers are the same today as when I was first asked many years ago. Probably the number one reason that a business fails is *undercapitalization*. Anyone going into business should have a cash reserve available in case it takes longer than projected to get the project off the ground. If you barely have enough financial resources to launch your business, what will you do when the unpredictable happens?

Perhaps the first thing one should consider is, is there a need for the product or service you are introducing? Are there enough people who want it, to make your business profitable? What is the *best* that can happen? What is the *worst* that can happen? Can you live with the *worst* thing? For instance, if you were not as successful as you anticipated, would you lose your home to foreclosure? Would you be unable to send your kids to college? Would you alienate your spouse, other relatives, and/or friends? Would there be any other life-changing consequences?

How important is success to you? Is it important enough to spend less time with your family and friends? We can't be all things to all people. Life is full of compromises. You can't be the *best* mother/father, the *best* wife/husband, the *best* daughter/son, the *best* in your business, all at one time. It's a good idea to make a list of priorities. Is your business important enough to work as hard and as long as is necessary to get the job done? Do you enjoy the work? Are you passionate about it? I have never met an athlete, musician, scientist, motion picture actor, or business executive who was inordinately successful who didn't love what he or she did and was passionate about it.

Is your business important enough to work as hard and as long as is necessary to get the job done?

When deciding to invest in your own business, it's wise to look to the leaders in that industry. How are they doing? Which one is the best in the category? Even if you can do as well as the best, will that be enough for you to be satisfied? There have been many successful losers, people who had great ideas, but the industry didn't provide enough opportunity to make their ideas worthwhile. Or, the product or service was so costly to produce that qualified buyers represented a very small market. So assess the opportunities and evaluate if you are prepared to take on the challenges they present.

There have been many successful losers, people who had great ideas, but the industry didn't provide enough opportunity to make their ideas worthwhile.

These are very basic things to consider, but you'd be surprised how many people are unaware or ignore the obvious. A case in point involves several people who have applied for a Jenny Craig franchise. When interviewing a prospective franchisee, we always asked the question, "Why do you want the franchise?" On several occasions, we received answers like, "I'm tired of being an employee. I want to be the boss so I can work the hours I want and be the one to tell others what to do." Needless to say, those people didn't get a franchise. We quickly informed them that that's not what we expect from our franchisees. As an owner, you can expect to work harder and longer than ever.

We can hire competent people to work in the centers. The best reason for selling a franchise is the level of confidence we have in knowing that the franchisee's heart and soul are in it. Anyone going into business thinking it's going to be the easy life is doomed to fail. People learn more from what they see than from what you tell them. If you're not willing to roll up your sleeves and do what's necessary to get the job done, you have two chances for your employees to do it: slim and none. Most successful executives I know are the first to arrive in the morning and the last to leave at night. That's why it's called *leadership*. As a leader, you need to demonstrate the behavior you expect from your employees.

I remember when I spoke to the graduating class at Harvard Business School in the early 1990s. Harvard had invited me because I was a member of The Committee 200, a group of entrepreneurial women throughout the world who either had started their own companies that had annual revenues of more than $10 million or who managed divisions that brought in more than $40 million in annual revenues. I was the only woman speaker on the Harvard panel, though, along with three male speakers.

As we broke for lunch, tables had been assembled with each speaker's name on a placard. The students were instructed to sit at whichever table they wanted. I expected to find only female students at my table. To my surprise, there was only one female and the rest were male students. What stands out in my mind are the answers I got when I went around the table asking what each one wanted to do after graduation. Many said they wanted to be stockbrokers. When I asked, "Why?" not one of them said, "Because that's what's exciting to me." I got answers from them like, "Because that's where the money is," or "Because my family can help me in that business." The one woman at the table was the only one who said, "I'm looking for something exciting and meaningful as a career."

We all know that financial success is a way of keeping score as to how well we're doing in the business world. But if money alone was the only reason to choose a career, there would be no teachers, no scientists, no nurses, no firemen, no policemen, along with many other professionals who have chosen their careers because they want to make a contribution for the good of us all, without the monetary glory. They are doing what they love, and loving what they do, and we are the beneficiaries of their choices.

Many very successful businesses evolved from the founder's love of the work. One case in point is Microsoft. Bill Gates started out working on projects that fascinated him and challenged him and eventually became his passion with computer technology. Debbie Fields began her business because she loved to bake cookies. J. K. Rowling became one of the most successful (and perhaps the richest) writers in history with her *Harry Potter* books, because she loves to write and does it well. Tiger Woods will soon be the richest man in sports (if he isn't already), because he loves the game of golf and he's good at it. When we do something better than anyone else in the category, whether it's sports, music, business, or anything else, the money will follow. People who choose a career for money alone have it backwards with little chance for success.

When I receive letters from people telling me of their great idea, the first thought that pops into my mind is, "I wonder how hard they're willing to work for it?" My experience has taught me that the journey from idea to financial success consists of "10 percent inspiration and 90 percent perspiration." There are millions of ideas generated every day. Yet, only a few reach fruition and become financial successes simply because the person wasn't willing to devote the time and effort necessary in research and development.

The Future of the Weight-Loss Industry

Most people today are looking for the shortcuts, both in business and in trying to lose weight. That's the reason so many diet pills and fat reducers are being sold. When the smoke clears, there is only one way to reduce and manage our weight: Eat less and exercise more. With every diet pill that is advertised, there is always a caveat, "It works only when combined with a healthy diet and exercise." Yet, we keep searching for the magic bullet, the thing that will work without any effort or discomfort.

Obesity is an ongoing concern in the United States, and it is getting more attention in the rest of the world, too. According to recent studies, obesity in the United States has increased almost 6 percent from 1998 to 1999. Sixty-one percent of Americans are considered overweight. Nearly 26 percent are viewed as obese, or weigh more than 30 pounds above a healthy weight range—a figure that has nearly doubled in the past two decades. What is particularly alarming is that 20 percent to 25 percent of children and adolescents are either overweight or at risk of becoming overweight. Obesity claims more than 300,000 lives each year, and it costs society an estimated $100 billion annually. Obesity is linked to at least 5 of the 10 leading causes of premature death: diabetes, hypertension, heart disease, stroke, and some forms of cancer. *Only smoking kills more people.*

Sixty-one percent of Americans are considered overweight. Nearly 26 percent are viewed as obese.

Our client success stories prove how a better approach to nutrition and exercise can change your life. For example, consider this story, of a 30-year-old man who became one of our clients:

There are many reasons why I finally decided to do something about my weight last January. But one of the most important reasons was I wanted to change the quality of my life.

While growing up, I tried diet after diet. One time, I lost 50 pounds, but put it back on—and then some. When I joined Jenny Craig, I weighed 290 pounds and was more than 100 pounds overweight. I couldn't walk and hold a conversation at the same time, and was always winded when I used the stairs at work. It got to the point where any type of physical activity was impossible.

A year and a half ago, I started a new job that required a lot of travel. It was very difficult and uncomfortable to fly, and I'd always feel embarrassed at the look on the face of the person who wound up being scrunched up next to me. Finally, my girlfriend convinced me it was time to do something about my weight . . . and she convinced me to go to Jenny Craig with her.

After two weeks on the program, everything just "clicked." I lost 140 pounds and it was one of the best things that ever happened to me. And it's not just because I'm a thinner person now, but because of what I've been able to accomplish. Every time I look ahead at a new step in life, I know I can achieve whatever I set my mind to.

One thing that amazes people is that I was able to lose weight while traveling all across the country. Jenny Craig really taught me how to eat—both when following their menu plans [at home] and while out on the road. I was able to entertain clients at restaurants and still lose weight.

> In the end, I'm just a person who is trying to make the best out of this game called life. And you know what? I DID IT!!!

A recent issue of *Time* magazine (August 25, 2003) featured an article on adolescent obesity: In China, 10 percent of adolescents and children are overweight, for the first time in history. In the United States, 37 percent of adolescents or children are overweight or obese. And in Europe, this number is 20 percent. So, we have twice as many at risk as Europe, and Europe has twice as many at risk as China, and this problem is increasing all the time. The article describes how obesity has changed the whole physical configuration of children, placing them at risk for life-threatening diseases.

So effective weight-loss management is needed even more than in the previous 20 years, because there are far more potential clients coming through the pipeline, and unless something is done about it—which I don't see happening on an international scale—we're going to have far more obese adults than ever before. The *Time* article said that more children are going to die before their parents.

Moreover, if a child's parents are overweight or obese, that child has an 80 percent chance of being overweight, too. And that's not just genetics at work; it's also *environment*, because so many children don't eat properly. Parents are not only their kids' role models, they're also *preparing* the foods that will contribute to their child's obesity.

I think genetics gives you a tendency to follow in your parents' footsteps, but it doesn't mean you have to. For example, if your parents were diabetic, you're predisposed to get diabetes, but if you have the proper lifestyle and take medication, you might not develop it. Genetics plays a role, but it's not the only predictor of what your outcome will be.

I feel such a strong need to help these children; it is the reason our company did some marketing to teens and children, but we didn't do much because it represented only a small portion of our clientele. Our advertising budget went only so far; we couldn't spend, say, 50 percent of the budget to capture only 10 percent of the market—that didn't make sense. But we did have programs for them, and we promoted them through the clients who came in. We talked to our clients about their kids, and we recruited children and adolescents through their parents, as long as the kids were at least 13 years old.

Young people today are already at a disadvantage because physical education classes have been eliminated from many schools' curricula. With computer time, video games, and TV demanding so much of their time, many children are getting very little exercise. Planning active outings that include swimming, biking, or just walking, and participating in sports like tennis, touch football, and soccer are both beneficial exercise and fun for the whole family.

Parents Should Teach Their Children about Nutrition

I look forward to the day when people care enough about their health and embrace life enough to make the few changes to their lifestyles that will ensure them a longer, healthier, and happier life span. The sad thing is that unless we make the decision to do so, our children will also be influenced by our poor decisions. Often I receive letters from parents asking what they can do to help their children avoid the weight challenges that have plagued them all through their lives. They ask questions like, "Is obesity genetic?" or "Should I force my child to eat things they don't like when I know it's healthy for them to do so?" I tell them to model the behavior they expect from their children.

For a long time there has been controversy over nature versus nurture. Sure, genetic programming plays an important role in the physical makeup of an individual, but there have been numerous studies that prove that even identical twins who have been separated as infants will not necessarily weigh the same throughout their youth. Just because offspring are genetically predisposed to a particular disease doesn't mean they will get that disease. It only means that there is a high percentage that they will have the disease if they don't try to prevent it from happening either through lifestyle changes or medication.

We all choose foods that we've gotten used to eating. For instance, in France, there are foods and portion sizes that are pretty standard for most natives. In Italy, there are different foods that are standards on the daily menu. Now, if French children grow up in Italy, they learn to eat like the Italians; conversely, if Italian children grow up in France, they learn to eat like the French. So there's no question that environment plays a critical role in eating behavior.

We have a responsibility to our children to introduce them to a healthy way of eating at an early age. Children learn more from what they see than from what we tell them. If we tell them to eat certain foods and we eat different foods, they will perceive their food as kid stuff, and they will resent it. On the other hand, if we practice what we preach, and eat the same healthy foods we tell them to eat, we will be setting the right example.

> We have a responsibility to our children
> to introduce them to a healthy
> way of eating at an early age.

For example, children today eat far too much sugar. Parents who serve rich desserts at every meal are training their children to expect that every meal should end with dessert. Offering them fruit at an early age instead of rich desserts trains them to make healthier choices. Learning to read labels is important, because there is so much sugar in some processed foods. Parents who are constantly eating processed snack foods are training their children to do the same.

Many of our clients have realized this on their own. Susan Prassas, a client of our Santa Monica center, wrote a letter to us confirming this:

> I was 35, a homemaker and gaining weight. My goal was to lose 20 pounds. I turned to Jenny Craig. Now I get a thrill when my daughter, Lauren, 4, and my son, Nicholas, 5, recite the food groups and talk about healthy eating. I feel I've done something for them, too.

Another mistake we make with our children is using food as a reward or punishment—for example, saying, "If you eat all your dinner, you can have dessert," or "If you don't do as I ask, you can't have any ice cream." So many young people with eating disorders have distorted views of food and its effect on them.

> ## Another mistake we make with our children is using food as a reward or punishment.

Many times, children learn these bad eating habits at home from well-meaning, loving parents. We don't all process information in the same way. So, by modeling the proper eating behavior for our children at an early age, and doing so without criticism, we are limiting the possibility that they will perceive hidden agendas behind food that is placed in front of them. Obesity among teenagers has reached epidemic proportions, as noted in the aforementioned *Time* magazine article. That doesn't mean that it's too late for us to have a meaningful impact on their future and overall health.

We owe it to our children to take positive action before they become obese adults with serious health problems. We can't do it with criticism, preaching, or threats.

We, as parents, have to make the same changes in our lifestyle that we expect our children to make. We must do so without open complaint of deprivation of previous favorite foods that we had become accustomed to eating, foods that we know were unhealthy when eaten in large quantities. Saying things like "I really miss my chocolate bars" gives children the impression that changing eating behavior is about doing without. There are no bad foods. *Moderation is key.* Learning to make the right food choices in the right portion size, along with regular exercise and activity is the key to weight management.

Making healthful lifestyle changes along with your children, and doing it with enthusiasm while putting forth a happy face, will send the message to your children that the change not only is good for us but it's fun and it tastes just as good as or better than the unhealthy foods. The old adage "Don't do as I do, do as I say" doesn't have credibility with children today. You must ask yourself, "How important is my and my children's health to me? Is it important enough to make a few changes that will benefit us all?" You are the only one who can truly answer that question.

Final Thoughts

"I can't wait for tomorrow."

I never intended for this book to be a swan song. From the beginning, I have viewed the events thus far as only the first phase of my life. As I said in the Introduction, this book started as a journal I began writing at the request of my children. There are still so many things I want to do and see—things and places I hope will be grist for the mill when writing accounts of my future experiences.

Some of the things I had planned for this past year included a walking trip to Puglia, Italy, with my daughters and a couple of friends; a trip to Paris with my oldest granddaughter, who had never been to Paris before; and a trip to Santa Fe with friends (my first visit there). I also planned to take up golf. I am happy to say that I have done all of those things. I have scheduled a series of golf lessons and hopefully they will uncover any possibility that I will be able to play well enough to enjoy the game. Our trip to Puglia was wonderful: It's a part of Italy I had never seen before and I enjoyed exploring every mile of it. Each day we walked through hills covered with wild poppies, whose vivid color created a Monet-like canvas that made our hearts beat a little faster. The coastline of the

Adriatic was breathtaking as we walked precariously along its edge. And, the food, oh my, the food was delicious!

My trip to Paris with Sydney, my oldest granddaughter, who's now 16, was a delight. We visited all the places of interest, including all the museums, Napoleon's tomb, Giverney (Monet's home), Van Gogh's gravesite and the churches he painted as well as the room where he died, the Eiffel Tower, Versailles, and L'Arc de Triomphe; and of course we managed to get a little shopping done. We ate at wonderful restaurants, feasting on delicious creations that the French are famous for.

Last year, my daughters and I also visited Ground Zero for my first look at the remnants of the worst disaster in U.S. history. I was young when President Franklin Roosevelt spoke the words, "This is a day that will live in infamy" on the day Pearl Harbor was attacked. He was right: We will never forget that day when every radio in this country blasted the news of the attack. But there was no TV then, and our minds could not quite conjure up the true impact of that horrible event until we saw it on the big screen long after it happened. By contrast, the visual images of the twin tower events of September 11, 2001—the devastation created, the lives that were tragically affected—we all watched *as it was happening*. Those images will permeate every cell in our bodies, our minds for the rest of our lives. Visiting that mass of rubble and reading the messages left by loved ones stirred emotions so overwhelming that I find it difficult to comprehend how the survivors are coping with their loss. My heart goes out to each one of them.

I shudder every time I think about that morning: I was in Sun Valley, watching the events unfold just as I turned on the *Today* show. I thought I was watching a promo for an upcoming movie. I was visiting a friend, expecting to enjoy a relaxing weekend. We spent most of the weekend watching and weeping as the realization evolved that the United States was under attack by evil forces.

If we ever doubted it before, that single event should have convinced us all that the United States and its people are the greatest in the world. The many acts of heroism and assistance, along with unprecedented generosity, showed the rest of the world how we pull together in times of crisis. Americans are a peculiar lot. We can openly criticize each other, publicly complain about taxes, laws, racism, sexism, politics, government policies, and sometimes be downright mean to each other, but, when an outsider attacks us, our national grievances become secondary. We behave as one family pulling together, protecting each other, united in a common cause. I am so proud of our country and its people! It's no wonder that so many people from other countries want to live here. Because it is so great, it engenders envy and jealousy by those who have never known such privileges. That's the bad news that causes us to be a little more cautious, a little more suspicious and aware of potential dangers. In spite of predictions, I hope one day soon we can return to the America we all shared before September 11.

On Achieving Success in Business and Living a Balanced Life

My life has been full in so many ways. I hope that in some small way others have benefited by the work that I chose, the relationships I have enjoyed with my husband, family, Jenny Craig clients, and the many friends whose friendship has meant so much to me over the years. If there has been one message, one phrase, one word that inspired them to be all that they can be and to view each day as another opportunity to do something meaningful, then the time I spent writing this journal will not have been wasted.

- *On taking risks:* Never risk more than you can afford to lose.
- *On starting a new business:* It's never too late. The factors that make a business successful have nothing to do with

199

chronological age. Assess your priorities and prepare yourself. There is no substitute for experience.

- *On success:* Be willing to do whatever it takes to get the job done. To be an effective leader you must demonstrate the behavior you expect from those you lead.

- *On persistence:* Don't readily accept the words "It can't be done." Continue to look for other ways of doing it. Be willing to spend the time and effort to be successful in your endeavors.

- *On working with a partner:* Make sure the skills of each of you complement the other's. Have clearly defined areas of responsibility.

- *On company size:* There are many benefits to keeping the corporate staff small. A small group can better communicate, make quicker decisions, and function better as a team.

- *On effective delegation:* Never assign to your employees a job that's impossible to accomplish. It not only limits their chances for success, but it also can damage their confidence and impair their self-image and self-worth.

- *On succession planning:* Work hard to duplicate yourself. You can advance in the corporate world only when you have a qualified replacement. Never feel threatened by those who work for you who have equal talents; they can only make you look better.

- *Demographics and psychographics:* Know the market you are trying to attract. If yours is a business appealing to women, you'd better have a woman included in important decisions. Women understand other women.

- *On selecting a career path:* Find something you love doing. The things we love doing we usually do well. When you do something better than anyone else in the category, position and fortune will follow.

- *On employee value:* Any business is simply four walls and people. No matter how great your product or service is, without good people delivering it, you have nothing.

- *On weight management:* Managing your weight is part of body health maintenance. It is not a one-time, short-term effort. It requires commitment, periodic assessment, and lifestyle adjustment when necessary.

- *On family-run business:* The most important thing to consider is whether working so closely with relatives is going to damage the family as a unit. Do the personalities and skills complement each other? Once you have answered that, it's important to have clearly defined roles for each family member. Try to discuss business matters at the office only—make family gatherings a time for fun and friendship.

- *On hiring:* During the 1990s we were all impressed by the applicants with MBAs. As we found out later, people who have grown up in a company can far outperform those with impressive academic credentials. Don't be afraid to go with your gut when an applicant has less formal schooling than others who apply.

- *On the value of hard work:* While attending a seminar years ago I heard a quote that has become somewhat of a mantra with me: "It's what you do when you don't *have to* that determines what you will become." Always do a little more than what is expected and you will be noticed and rewarded.

- *On decision-making:* Sometimes making a decision can be difficult. When I'm faced with a dilemma, I use the Ben Franklin technique of listing all the reasons for doing it on one side of a page, and on the other side I list all the reasons for *not* doing it. I have found that one side will always outweigh the other, thus giving me a guidepost toward a decision.

Finally, now that I reflect on my life thus far I am reminded of some lessons I've learned over the years through personal experience and the wisdom of others who have graced my life.

- *Things* aren't important to happiness; *people* are. Sometimes we get so caught up in the pursuit of, and acquisition of things, that we fail to devote enough time to developing good and lasting relationships that nourish our spirit, bring joy to our hearts, and chronicle events throughout our lifetime.

- We can't be *all* things to *all* people. The important thing is to be your true authentic self. Trying to design your life by someone else's blueprint creates disappointment and frustration for both parties.

- We alone are responsible for our actions. Life is filled with choices. It's the choices we make each day that determine in what direction our life will take us. Sometimes we make poor choices. Placing blame on other people or things does little to alter the results.

- *Never* postpone pleasure. Tomorrow is an abstraction; we do not know what capricious agenda is waiting, undetected, to change our plans. Enjoy, without guilt, each and every thing that brings pleasure to you.

- Forgotten I love you's can never be redeemed as sincere feelings when they are stored up, only to be spoken in the winter of our life or as a final good-bye. Make it a practice to say it often to all those who share your life, whose love is yours for the taking.

- Make your *actions* speak louder than your words. Saying "I love you" and failing to demonstrate to your loved ones that those are not just empty words, has little or no meaning. A helping hand, a hug, a kiss, a phone call, a letter, or a visit speak much louder than words alone.

- Don't look back in *anger*, don't look forward in *fear*, look around in *awareness*. Learn to appreciate all the good things about your life, the things you are most proud of. Don't dwell on the past, focusing on what could have been or why things turned out the way they did. Never be afraid to take a chance. Remember *no risk, no reward*. None of us have a crystal ball to tell us what the future holds. All we can do is try to make intelligent choices and believe they will result in a positive outcome.

- I've learned that the *quantity* of life has no correlation to the *quality* of life. If we want quality we must be prepared to invest time and attention to the things that are proven essentials in reaching that goal. Things like healthy diet, regular exercise, body-health maintenance, loving relationships, laughter, and fun improve life dramatically. Genetics can allow you to live *longer* but only you can make your life *better*.

- If there is anything better or more joyful than a grandchild's smile as he/she looks into your eyes and says, "Nana, I love you," I can't wait to discover it.

- I've learned that everyone has a soul mate somewhere, and if we're lucky enough to find them, to share our life with, then we are more fortunate than most. I thank God every day for allowing me to find mine. Sid has enriched my life in more ways than I can count. I know tomorrow will be even brighter, because he will be there to share it with me.

There are many who have had a more *exciting* life than mine has been thus far. But I don't believe there are many who have enjoyed life more, lived it with more *gusto*, more purpose and determination, none more fulfilled, none who have cherished their friendships more and have been more grateful for the many blessings that God has bestowed, than I have. I can't wait for tomorrow because each day brings new wonderments of life to be enjoyed and cherished.

Index

Victorian Economic Council
(VEC), 95
Vision, importance of, 2
Vitamins, 88–89, 98–99

Walking, health benefits of,
173
Wedding memories, 24
Weight gain, reasons for, 109–111
Weight loss, generally:
education, 34–35
health benefits of, 125
psychological impact, 35–36
Weight-loss/weight-management
industry:
changes in, 3
future directions in, 189–193
legal challenges for, 152–153
Weight management, 83–84,
109–110, 201

Weight schedules, 123–124
Weight Watchers, 71, 90, 122,
124, 153, 177–179
Weinger, Duayne, 106–107,
125–126, 133–134,
171–172
Weinger, Michelle Rae Bourcq,
25–27, 31, 33–34, 36, 51, 57,
94, 103–108, 117, 125–126,
133, 140, 171–172
Weinger, Remington, 125
Weinger, Sydney, 125,
198
Weinger, Zachary, 125
Williams, Cindy, 122
Willpower, 113
Woods, Tiger, 189
Work ethic, 6, 8–9, 156,
201
Wyden, Ron, 153